GULLUH FUH OONUH

(GULLAH FOR YOU)

GULLUH FUH OONUH

(GULLAH FOR YOU)

A Guide to the Gullah Language

Virginia Mixson Geraty

SANDLAPPER PUBLISHING CO., INC.
ORANGEBURG, SOUTH CAROLINA

© 1997 Virginia Mixson Geraty

Third Printing, 2006

All rights reserved.

Published by Sandlapper Publishing Co., Inc.
Orangeburg, South Carolina 29115

Manufactured in the United States of America

Library of Congress Cataloging-in-Publication Data

Geraty, Virginia Mixson.
    Gullah Fuh Oonuh : a Gullah/English guide / by Virginia
Mixson Geraty.
        p. cm.
    ISBN 0-87844-137-9
    1. Sea Islands Creole dialect—Dictionaries—English. I. Title.
PM7875.G8G47   1997
427'.975799—dc21   97-31363
                                                                       CIP
ISBN 13: 978-0-87844-137-2

Fuh

me sistuh
me chillun
me gran'
en'
me great-gran'

Preface

One of my most pleasant and significant memories is that of my grandmother's kitchen during the 1920 Christmas holiday at her home on Yonges Island, South Carolina. It was there I first heard Gullah, an experience that marked the beginning of a love affair with this language—an immediate infatuation, which was to intensify through the years.

The house had been decorated in traditional Lowcountry holiday style, with smilax, mistletoe, and holly. The Christmas tree was resplendent, and on its top sat a smiling angel, silently enforcing the "Don't open" messages written on the packages piled underneath. A cheerful fire burned and crackled in the fireplace, where . . . yes . . . stockings were hung!

Despite the appeal of the Christmas spirit in the living room, like the children of Hamelin, I was drawn to an enchanting sound coming from the kitchen—a voice speaking or singing in a strange language.

I do not remember when my father began reading to me, but every evening after dinner he would read stories and poems from a thick, brown book—no silly rhymes or nonsense. I was in elementary school before I learned that *dogs laugh when cows jump over the moon.* From my father's book I had heard about the Pied Piper at an early age. If there was a piper in Grandmother's kitchen, I must tell my father!

Drawn to the kitchen, I stood in the doorway unnoticed for a few minutes while a brown lady moved about singing very strange words. Suddenly she stopped singing and spoke to me. "Mek oonuh duh stan' dey dey, chile? Seddown yuh en' hab uh cookie." I had no idea what she had said, but when she gave me a cookie, I knew I had a friend.

I was captivated by her speech, and through the years my fascination with her Gullah language has continued to grow. Because of my work toward the preservation of Gullah, in 1995 I received the honorary degree of Doctor of Humane Letters from the College of Charleston, Charleston, South Carolina.

Introduction

My purpose in preparing this work is twofold. I have received numerous requests for information about the Gullah language. And, while this book is my answer to these requests, the primary purpose in all my work with Gullah is to increase public awareness of the language and generate interest in the preservation of this significant linguistic contribution of the African American people to America's heritage.

Gullah is both the name of a people and the name of the language these people speak. This language attained creole status during the mid 1700s and was learned and used by the second generation of African Americans as their mother tongue.

Growing from African roots, planted in American soil, and nourished by various English dialects, a linguistic analysis of the Gullah language will determine that the greater part of its lexicon is traceable to English words. However, the sentence structure, intonation, and stress reveal a clear correspondence to the languages spoken on the west coast of Africa.

Since Gullah is an English-derived creole, the English alphabet is used to represent its sounds. Most of the letters used in the spelling of Gullah words have the same sounds that are used to form English words. However, there are changes in the sounds of some letters, some consonant shifts, and some sounds that are peculiar to Gullah and bear a marked resemblance to African langauges, particularly Krio spoken in Sierra Leone.

Gulluh Fuh Oonuh has been designed for students of all ages and academic levels. In its preparation, confusing phonetic symbols have been avoided and a pronunciation key has been provided according to the *Oxford American Dictionary* (Oxford, NY: Oxford Press, 1980). Other than the apostrophe, no diacritical marks have been used. This is to avoid mistakes in spelling and pronunciation should these marks become confused with the apostrophe, which is so important to the orthography and pronunciation of Gullah. This apostrophe is used to show the omission of a letter, a word or a group of words. NEVER does it show possession. The other use of the apostrophe is to show word boundary, as "mek'um" meaning make them. The two words are pronounced as one.

Pronunciation is shown in parenthesis below each entry. Syllables are separated by hyphens, and those spoken with stress are written in capital letters. Since Gullah is an English-derived language, there are many English letters that Gullah speakers pronounce and use according to Standard English. These words are, obviously, not included in this guide. However, English words that are used with Gullah words to form idiomatic expressions are included, and the expressions are listed alphabetically.

Gulluh Fuh Oonuh should prove to be a valuable tool for students and researchers by providing information and, at the same time, assuring them that

Gullah is a legitimate creole language, and one that should be preserved as a significant part of our American heritage.

Pronunciation Key

Unless otherwise indicated,

a is pronounced as in bat
aa as in baa
b as in boy
c as in cat
d as in dug
e as in egg
ee as in see
f as in fit
g as in gun
h as in hat
i as in it
j as in jam
k as in kin
l as in leg
m as in me
n as in net
o as in own
p as in paper

r as in read
s as in see
t as in tea
th is omitted
> NOTE: "th" becomes "d" in den (then), dem (them), dose (those). The "h" is dropped in most cases. Thin becomes t'in, thief becomes t'ief.

u as in use
v is omitted
> NOTE: "v" becomes "b" in berry (very) or "w" in wine (vine).

w as in wool
y as in yes
z as in zebra

Abbreviations

Small letters following the pronunciation denote the part of speech.

n.	noun
pron.	pronoun
PN.	proper noun
adj.	adjective
adv.	adverb
v.	verb
prep.	preposition
conj.	conjuncton
inter.	interjection
id.	idiomatic expression

Entry Layout

Each entry is followed by a Gullah sentence, which illustrates that entry, and the Standard English translation of that sentence.

> *Example:* aa'k
> (AAK) *n.* ark/-s
> "Mistuh Noruh bil' de aa'k."
> (Mister Noah built the ark.)

GULLUH FUH OONUH

(GULLAH FOR YOU)

A

aa'bay
(AA-bay) *n.* abbey/-s
"Uh wu'k tuh de aa'bay."
(I work at the abbey.)

aa'bitrate
(AA-bit-rate) *v.* arbitrate/-s/
-ed, arbitrating; settle/-s/-ed,
settling
"De pastuh en' de elduh
aa'bitrate de 'spute."
(The pastor and the elders
settled the dispute.)

aabut
(AA-but) *n.* abbot/-s
"De aabut de aa'bay ob'shay."
(The abbot is the abbey
overseer.)

aa'ch
(AA-ch) *n.* arch/-es
"De cyaa'pentuh done bil' de
aa'ch."
(The carpenter has built the
arch.)

aa'ch
(AA-ch) *v.* arch/-es/-ed/-ing
"De cat duh aa'ch 'e back."
(The cat is arching its back.)

aacit
(AA-cit) *n.* acid
"'E tas'e shaa'p, sukkuh aacit."
(It has a sharp taste, like acid.)

aa'gyfy
(AA-gy-fy) *v.* argue/-s/-d,
arguing
"De gal aa'gyfy wid 'e ma."
(The girl argued with her
mother.)

aa'gymu't
(AA-GY-mut) *n.* argument/-s
"Dey ax de pastuh fuh settle
de aa'gymu't."
(They asked the pastor to settle
the argument.)

aa'k
(AAK) *n.* ark/-s
"Mistuh Noruh bil' de aa'k."
(Mister Noah built the ark.)

aa'm
(AAM) *n.* arm/-s
"De man aa'm bruk."
(The man's arm is broken.)

aa'm
(AAM) *v.* arm/-s
"'E aa'm wid uh two-time-one-
gun."
(He is armed with a double-
barreled shotgun.)

aa'ms
(AAMS) *n.* alms
"De po' man gone de aa'bay
fuh ax fuh aa'ms."
(The poor man went to the
abbey to ask for alms.)

aa'my
(AA-my) *n.* army, armies
"Me niece jine de aa'my."
(My nephew joined the army.)
NOTE: "NIECE" IS THE GULLAH
WORD FOR ONE'S BROTHER'S OR
SISTER'S SON OR DAUGHTER.
"NEPHEW" IS NOT USED.

aamynishun
(AA-MY-ni-shun) *n.* ammunition
"De sodjuh nyuse up all de aamynishun."
(The soldiers used up all the ammunition.)

abbuhtize
(ab-buh-TIZE) *v.* advertise/-d, advertising
"Us abbuhtize we faa'm fuh sell."
(We advertised our farm for sale.)

aabuhtizemu't
(aab-uh-TIZE-mut) *n.* advertisement/-s
"De abbuhtizemu't een de nyusepapuh."
(The advertisement is in the newspaper.)

ab'nue
(AB-nue) *n.* avenue/-s
"Uh gal duh peruse 'long de ab'nue."
(A girl is strolling along the avenue.)

ack
(ACK) *v.* act/-s/-ed/-ing
"'E yent sick; dat de pyo' ack."
(He isn't sick; he is simply acting.)

ack'natchul
(ack-NAT-chul) *id.* act natural; act according to instinct
"'Co'se de dog t'ief de chickin; 'e ack'natchul."
(Of course the dog stole the chicken; he was acting according to his natural instinct.)

acksident
(ack-si-DENT) *n.* accident/-s
"Uh acksident bin hab tuh Main Skreet."
(There was an accident on Main Street.)

ackybat
(ACK-y-bat) *n.* acrobat/-s
"'Nuf ackybat bin een de sukkus."
(Many acrobats were in the circus.)

acquaintun
(ac-QUAIN-tun) *v.* acquainted
"Uh yent dat acquaintun wid'um."
(I am not that acquainted with them.)

adduh
(AD-duh) *n.* adder/-s
"Dat bin uh adduh snake."
(That snake was an adder.)

adwance
(ad-WANCE) *n.* advance/-s
"'E ax please kin 'e hab adwance on 'e pay."
(He asked if he could please have an advance on his pay.)

adwantage
(ad-WAN-tage) *n.* advantage/-s
"Rowboss hab adwantage mo'nuh fiel' han'."
(A row boss has more advan-

tages than a field hand.)

af'
(AF) *adv.* aft; rear
"Set tuh de af' de boat."
(Sit to the back of the boat.)

Aff'ikin
(AFF-I-kin) *PN.* African/-s
"'Nuf Aff'ikin come tuh de New Wu'll'."
(Many Africans came to the New World.)

Aff'iky
(AFF-I-ky) *PN.* Africa
"Dem come f'um Aff'iky."
(They came from Africa.)

agguhnize
(AG-guh-nize) *v.* agonize/-s/-ed, agonizing; fret/-s/-ed/-ing
"De 'ooman agguhnize wid de mis'ry."
(The woman is suffering with pain.)
"Ma duh agguhnize 'kase de dog nyam de aig."
(Mother is fretting because the dog ate the eggs.)

agguhnize me bone
(AG-guh-nize me BONE) *id.* become exhausted, bone weary
"Uh wu'k 'tell uh agonize me bone."
(I have worked until I am exhausted.)

aggywate
(AG-GY-wate) *v.* aggravate/-s/-ed, aggravating
"Ebram lady aggywate tummuch."
(Ebram's wife aggravates him too much.)

aig
(AIG) *n.* egg/-s
"All de aig hatch out."
(All the eggs hatched.)

aig
(AIG) *v.* urge/-s/-d, urging
"'E aig'um on 'tell dem fight."
(He urged them on until they fought.)

ainjul
(AIN-jul) *n.* angel/-s
"De ainjul repeah tuh Mary."
(The angel appeared to Mary.)

alldo'
(all-DO) *conj.* although
"Uh gwine alldo' uh feel sawtuh po'ly."
(I'm going although I don't feel very well.)

alltime
(ALL-time) *adv.* always
"Dem alltime gone chu'ch."
(They have always gone to church.)

alltuh
(ALL-tuh) *v.* alter/-s/-ed/-ing
"De ob'shay alltuh de hog."
(The overseer altered the hog.)

alltwo
(all-TWO) *adj.* both
"'E bu'n alltwo 'e han'."
(He burned both his hands.)

all ub uh sudd'n
(all-ub-uh-SUDD-'n) *adv.* all of a sudden; suddenly
"All ub uh sudd'n de gal hice de chune."
(Suddenly the girls began to sing.)

ambrelluh
(AM-brel-luh) *n.* umbrella/-s
"Ma cya' 'e ambrelluh 'long'um."
(Mother carried her umbrella with her.)

anch
(ANCH) *n.* ant/-s
"De anch 'ting'um."
(The ants stung them.)

an'i'on
(AN-i'on) *n.* andiron/-s
"An'i'on hol' de 'ood een de chimbly."
(Andirons hold the wood in the fireplace.)

ankyhall
(ANK-Y-hall) *n.* alcohol
"Ankyhall weh 'e lib."
(Alcohol is his chief concern.)

anudduh
(a-NUD-duh) *adj.* another
"Anudduh gal bin dey."
(Another girl was there.)

ansuh
(AN-suh) *n.* answer; message, particularly one that requires a response
"Ma sen' ansuh."
(Mother sent a message.)

ap'
(AP) *adv.* apt; likely
"'E yent ap' fuh do'um."
(He isn't likely to do it.)

appuhratux
(ap-puh-RAT-ux) *n.* apparatus; instrument
"Uh sho' ent know how dat tallyfon appuhratus wu'k."
(I surely don't know how that telephone instrument works.)

ap'un
(A-pun) *n.* apron/-s
"De gal tayre 'e ap'un."
The girl tore her apron.

ashish
(ASH-ish) *n.* ash/-es
"De ashish haffuh cya' out."
(The ashes have to be carried out.)

attacktid
(at-TACK-tid) *v.* attack/-s/-ed/-ing
"Uh dog attacktid de 'ooman."
(A dog attacked the woman.)

attuh
(AT-tuh) *adv.* after
"Gally gone home attuh brekwus."
(Gally went home after breakfast.)

attuh-gun-shoot
(at-tuh-GUN-shoot) *id.* after the Civil War
"Freedum come een attuh-gun-shoot."
(Freedom began after the Civil War.)

attuhr'um
(AT-TUH-rum) *adv.* after him/
her/it/them
"De boy gone attuhr'um."
(The boy went after them.)

attuhw'ile
(at-tuh-WILE) *adv.* after a
while
"Attuhw'ile Uh gwine home."
(After a while I'm going
home.)

auttymobile
(aut-ty-mo-BILE) *n.* automo-
bile/-s
"Uh kin dribe de auttymobile?"
(May I drive the automobile?)

awready
(aw-READ-Y) *adv.* already
"Uh done awready ax'um."
(I have already asked them.)

awright
(aw-RIGHT) *adv.* all right
"De mis'ry bin hab'um, 'cep'
'e awright now."
(He suffered much pain, but he
is all right now.)

ax
(AX) *v.* ask/-s/-ed/-ing
"Ma ax kin 'e hab de tettuh."
(Mother asked if she could
have the potato.)

B

baa'
(BAA) *v.* bar/-s, barred,
barring
"Baa' de do'!"
(Bar the door!)

baa'b
(BAAB) *n.* barb
"De baa'b jook een 'e foot."
(The barb stuck in his foot.)

baa'beque
(BAA-be-QUE) *v.* barbecue/-s/
-d, barbecuing
"De hog done baa'beque."
(The hog is barbecued already.)

baa'buh
(BAA-buh) *n.* barber/-s
"De baa'buh shabe 'e head."
(The barber shaved his head.)

baa'bwyuh
(baab-WY-UH) *n.* barb wire
"De fench mek ub
baa'bwyuh."
(The fence is made of barb
wire.)

baa'gun
(BAA-gun) *v.* bargain/-s/-ed/
-ing
"Dem duh baa'gun fuh buy de
hog."
(They are bargaining for the
hog.)

baa'k
(BAAK) *n.* bark
"Pine baa'k good fuh kindle
fiah."
(Pine bark is good to start a
fire.)

baa'k
(BAAK) *v.* bark/-s/-ed/-ing

"All de dog, dem, duh baa'k."
(All the dogs are barking.)

baa'n
(BAAN) *n.* barn/-s
"Two cow een de baa'n."
(There are two cows in the barn.)

baa'nyaa'd
(BAAN-yaad) *n.* barnyard/-s
"De nex' cow een de baa'nyaa'd."
(The other cow is in the barnyard.)

babbidge
(BABB-idge) *n.* babbit; metal coins used as exchange in plantation commissaries
"Us spen' all we babbidge tuh de sto'."
(We spent all our babbit at the store.)

back'ood
(BACK-ood) *n.* backwoods
"Dat gal lib tuh de back'ood."
(That girl lives in the backwoods.)

bactize
(BAC-tize) *v.* baptize/-s/-d, baptizing
"Two 'ooman git bactize."
(Two women were baptized.)

bactizum
(bac-TIZ-um) *n.* baptism/-s
"De bactizum bin hab tuh de Toogoodoo Ribbuh."
(The baptism took place in the Toogoodoo River.)

baddle-cake
(BAD-DLE-cake) *n.* batter-cake; pancake
"De chile nyam t'ree baddle-cake."
(The child ate three batter-cakes.)

bad mout'
(BAD mout) *v.* bad mouth; curse verbally or put a spell on someone
"De man wife bad mout'um tummuch."
(The man's wife cursed him too much.)

baig
(BA-ig) *v.* beg/-s, begged, begging
"Dey baig'um fuh gone."
(They begged them to go.)

bakin
(BAY-kin) *n.* bacon
"Ma gone sto' fuh buy bakin."
(Mother went to the store to buy bacon.)

'bandun
(BAN-dun) *v.* abandon/-s/-ed/-ing
"'Bram done 'bandun 'e fambly."
(Abraham has already abandoned his family.)

barril
(BAR-RIL) n. barrel/-s
"Pa buy uh barril ub flowuh las' munt'."
(Father bought a barrel of flour last month.)

bawn
(BAWN) *v.* born
"De chile bin bawn de two week done gone."
(The child was born two weeks ago.)

bay'nit
(BAY-nit) *n.* bayonet/-s
"Uh jook'um wid de muskick bay'nit."
(I stabbed him with the musket bayonet.)

bayre
(BAYRE) *v.* bear/-s, bore, bearing
"Sistuh bayre 'e mis'ry bedout mek complain."
(Sister bore her pain without complaining.)

bayre
(BAYRE) *adj.* bare; not covered
"'E bayre feet."
(He is barefooted.)

bayre
(BAYRE) *n.* bear/-s
"Uh bayre dey dey een de 'ood."
(There is a bear there in the woods.)
NOTE: THE USE OF "DEY DEY" DENOTES "RIGHT THERE," AT THAT PARTICULAR LOCATION.

beat du't
(BEET dut) *id.* run fast enough to cause dust to rise
"'E beat du't tuh de big road."
(He ran as fast as he could to the highway.)

beat groun'
(BEET groun) *id.* run
"'E beat groun' tuh de sto'."
(He ran to the store.)

beat me time
(BEAT me TIME) *id.* indicates superior performance at a game or undertaking
"'E dance tuh beat me time."
(She danced much better than I did.)

beat me time
(BEAT me TIME) *interj.* an expression of disbelief or surprise
"Bina marri'd? Dat beat me time!"
(Bina got married? I can't believe it!)

beat stick
(BEAT STICK) *id.* keep time (for dancing) by beating two sticks together
"Buh Joe beat stick fuh de chillun dance."
(Brother Joe kept time by beating sticks together for the children to dance.)

bed chile
(BED chile) *n.* a child too young to sit alone
"De 'ooman hab uh bed child en' two yaa'd chillun.
(The woman has a child too young to sit up and two children old enough to play in the yard.)

bedout
(be-DOUT) *prep.* without
"'E gone bedout 'e mek 'e mannus."
(He went without saying goodbye.)
NOTE: "MEK 'E MANNUS" MEANS TO ACT IN A POLITE MANNER.

beebuh
(BEE-buh) *n.* beaver/-s
"Beebuh bil' dam een de ribbuh."
(Beavers build dams in the river.)

befo'foot
(be-FO-foot) *n.* front foot/feet
"De dog hu't alltwo 'e befo'foot."
(The dog hurt both his front feet.)

behabe
(be-HABE) *v.* behave/-s/-d, behaving
"De chillun behabe too bad."
(The children behaved very badly.)

behime
(be-HIME) *adv.* behind
"De hog behime de fench."
(The hog is behind the fence.)

'bejun'
(BE-jun) *adj.* obedient
"Dem chillun berry 'bejun'."
(Those children are very obedient.)

bekase
(be-KASE) *conj.* because
"'E yent wu'k bekase 'e sick."
(He isn't working because he is sick.)

bekasew'y
(BE-kase-wy) *conj.* [because why]; because; the reason being
"'E yent wu'k bekasew'y 'e hab de remonia."
(He didn't work because he had pneumonia.)

belluh
(BEL-luh) *v.* bellow/-s/-ed/-ing
"De alligettuh belluh same lukkuh bull."
(Alligators bellow just like bulls.)

belly pinch'um
(bel-ly PINCH-um) *id.* is/was hungry
"'E belly pinch'um."
(He was hungry.)

ben'
(BEN) *v.* bend/-s, bent, bending
"De cyaa't w'eel ben'."
(The cart's wheel is bending.)

benny
(BEN-ny) *n.* benne seed
"De bread mek wid benny een'um."
(The bread is made with benne seed.)

berry
(BER-ry) *adv.* very
"'Bram uh berry soon-man."
(Abraham is a very stylish

man.)
NOTE: BERRY AND WERRY ARE USED INTERCHANGEABLY.

berrywellden
(ber-ry-WELL-den) *id.* very well then
"Berrywellden, Uh gwine!"
(Very well then, I am going!)

bex
(BEX) *v.* vex/-es/-ed/-ing
"De boy bex 'e ma."
(The boy vexed his mother.)

bex hab'um
(bex HAB-um) *id.* anger has overcome him/her
"'E duh talk so bekase bex hab'um."
(She is saying that because she is extremely angry.)

bex 'long 'e mout'
(BEX long e mout) *id.* so mad he/she cursed
"'E tarrygate 'tell 'e bex 'long 'e mout.'"
(She was interrogated until she was so aggravated she cursed.)

bex 'long 'e yeye
(BEX long e yeye) *id.* so mad he/she cried
"'E tarrygate 'tell 'e bex 'long 'e yeye."
(She was interrogated until she was so mad she cried.)
NOTE: "YEYE" MEANING "EYE," SO SPELLED WHEN PRECEDED BY A VOWEL.

bex tek'um
(bex TEK-um) *id.* anger overcame him/her
"W'en de chickin t'ief, bex tek'um."
(When the chicken was stolen, she became infuriated.)

bidness
(BID-ness) *n.* business/-es
"Uh tell'um mus' min' 'e own bidness."
(I told him to mind his own business.)

big house
(BIG house) *n.* the main house on a plantation; the residence of the plantation owner
"Uh paa'ty bin hab tuh de big house."
(A party was held at the big house.)

big road
(BIG road) *n.* main road; highway/-s
"Uh shum come 'long de big road."
(I saw them coming along the highway.)

bile
(BILE) *v.* boil/-s/-ed/-ing
"Bile t'ree aig."
(Boil three eggs.)

bilin'
(BI-lin) *adj.* boiling
"Drap de aig een bilin' watuh."
(Drop the eggs in boiling water.)

billage
(BIL-lage) *n.* village/-s
"Dem lib tuh de billage."
(They live in the village.)

biluh
(BI-luh) *n.* boiler/-s
"De biluh 'pun'top de stobe."
(The boiler is on the stove.)

bimeby
(BIME-by) *adv.* by and by; after a while
"Bimeby Uh gwine home."
(After a while, I'm going home.)

bin
(BIN) *v.* been; was
"'E bin tuh we house yistiddy."
(He was at our house yesterday.)

bin fuh hab
(bin fuh HAB) *v.* was to have been held
"Uh picnic bin fuh hab Sat'd'y done gone, 'cep'm 'e wedduh."
(A picnic was to have been held last Saturday, but it rained.)

binnuh
(BIN-nuh) *id.* was a
"W'en Uh binnuh leetle chile, uh gone chu'ch."
(When I was a little child, I went to church.)

bite 'e meat
(bite e MEAT) *id.* sting, bite, pinch, or cut him/her
"Muskittuh bite 'e meat."
(The mosquitoes stung him.)

bittle
(BIT-tle) *n.* victual; food
"'E tell de chile mus' nyam de bittle."
(She told the child he must eat the food.)

blam
(BLAM) *v.* strike/-s, struck, striking
"Dem duh bil', 'kase uh yeddy'um duh blam nail."
(They are building, because I hear them driving nails.)
NOTE: *BLAM* IS TAKEN FROM THE SOUND MADE WHEN ONE OBJECT STRIKES ANOTHER, AS A HAMMER STRIKING A NAIL.

blan-b'long
(BLAN-blong) *id.* used to belong
"Dat house blan-b'long tuh me grum'pa."
(That house used to belong to my grandfather.)

b'leebe
(BLEEBE) *v.* believe/-s/-d, believing
"Uh b'leebe uh shum."
(I believe I see them.)

'bleege
(BLEEGE) *v.* oblige/-s/-d/ obliging
"Dey 'bleege'um duh min' de chillun."
(They are obliging them by

Virginia Mixson Geraty

minding the children.)

blessit
(BLES-sit) *adj.* blessed
"De blessit dead sleep duh de grabeyaa'd."
(The blessed dead sleep in the graveyard.)

bline
(BLINE) *n.* blind
"'E duh set een de bline duh wait fuh de duck."
(He is sitting in the blind waiting for the ducks.)

bline
(BLINE) *v.* blind/-s/-ed/-ing
"De light'n bline 'e yeye."
(The lightning blinded him.)

bline
(BLINE) *adj.* blind
"Jedus cyo' de bline man."
(Jesus cured the blind man.)

b'long
(BLONG) *v.* belong/-s/-ed/-ing
"De goat b'long tuh me bubbuh."
(The goat belongs to my brother.)

bloodynoun
(BLOOD-Y-noun) *n.* a large bullfrog having a loud bellow
"W'en de alligettuh belluh fuh rain, de bloodynoun jine'um."
(When the alligators bellow for rain, the big bullfrogs join them.)

bo'
(BO) *n.* boar/-s
"De mens gone fuh hunt bo'."
(The men have gone boar hunting.)

boa'd
(BOAD) *n.* board/-s
"De fench mek ub boa'd."
(The fence is made of boards.)

boa'd
(BOAD) *v.* board/-s/-ed/-ing
"Boa'd de boat; 'e time fuh gone!"
(Board the boat; it's time to go!)

bodduh
(BOD-duh) *v.* bother/-s/-ed/-ing
"De chillun bodduhr'um tummuch."
(The children bothered them too much.)
NOTE: THE MEDIAL "R" IN *BODDUHR'UM* IS ADDED FOR EUPHONY; IT HAS NO OTHER VALUE.

bodduhrashun
(bod-duh-RASH-un) *n.* an annoyance
"Dat squinch-owl uh bodduhrashun fuh true."
(That screech owl is truly an annoyance.)

bofe
(BOFE) *adj.* both
"Bofe de mens wu'k."
(Both men worked.)

bo'hog
(BO-hog) *n.* boar [hog]; wild hog; an uncastrated male hog
"Mus' don' fench-up bo'hog tuhgedduh."
(You must not put two male hogs in the same pen.)

bol'
(BOL) *adj.* bold
"Rokkoon bol', 'cep' fox bol' de mores'."
(Raccoons are bold, but foxes are bolder.)

bol'weeble
(bol-WEE-ble) *n.* boll weevil/-s
"'Nuf bol'weeble een de cotton."
(There are many boll weevils in the cotton.)

borruh
(BOR-RUH) *v.* borrow/-s/-ed/-ing
"'E come fuh borruh we ax."
(He came to borrow our ax.)

boun'
(BOUN) *v.* bound; determined
"'E boun' fuh tas'e de apple."
(She was determined to taste the apple.)

'bout
(BOUT) *prep.* about
"Dem gone 'bout dem bidness."
(They went about their business.)

bowdashus
(bow-DAY-shus) *adj.* audacious; bold
"'E bowdashus en' 'e too swonguh."
(He is audacious and very boastful.)

box-up
(BOX-up) *adj.* boxed up; closed like a box turtle
"'E mout' box-up; 'e dat bex."
(Her mouth is closed tightly like a turtle; she is that vexed.)

brabe
(BRABE) *adj.* brave
"De gal brabe fuh peruse de paa't duh middlenight."
(The girl is brave to walk the path at midnight.)

brawtus
(BRAW-tus) *n.* bonus/-es; extra; good measure
"Pa g'em uh fish fuh brawtus."
(Father gave them a fish for good measure.)

breas'
(BREAS) *n.* breast/-s
"Ma sabe de chickin breas' fuh de pastuh'."
(Mother saved the fried chicken breast for the pastor.)

bredduh
(BRED-duh) *n.* brother/-s
"De chu'ch bredduh gedduh fuh de meet'n'."
(The brothers of the church are gathering for the meeting.)

bredduh-law
(BRED-DUH-law) *n.* brother/-s-in-law
"Me bredduh-law gone tuh de paa'ty."
(My brothers-in-law went to the party.)

bred'ren
(BRED-ren) *n.* brethren
"All de bred'ren bin tuh de picnic."
(All the brethren were at the picnic.)

breeze
(BREEZE) *v.* breathe/-s/-d, breathing
"De col' hab me; Uh haa'dly'kin breeze."
(I have a cold; I can hardly breathe.)

brekwus'
(BREK-wus') *n.* breakfast/-s
"De chillun hab aig en' hom'ny fuh brekwus'."
(The children had egg and hominy for breakfast.)

brekwus'-swimp
(BREK-wus'-SWIMP) *n.* shrimp cooked in gravy
"Uh berry lub fuh nyam brekwus'-swimp en' hom'ny."
(I very much like to eat shrimp cooked in gravy and hominy.)

bresh
(BRESH) *n.* brush/-es
"Oonuh mus' nyuse uh bresh fuh clean de h'aa't'."
(You must use a brush to clean the hearth.)

bresh
(BRESH) *v.* brush/-es/-ed/-ing
"Bresh de buttuh 'cross de tettuh."
(Brush butter on the potato.)

bresh
(BRESH) *n.* bush/-es
"Blackberry bresh 'cratch de chile aa'm."
(Blackberry bushes scratched the child's arm.)

bress
(BRESS) *v.* bless/-es/-ed/-ing
"Pa bress de bittle."
(Father blessed the food.)

bre't'
(BRET) *n.* breath
"De boy run 'tell 'e loss 'e bre't'."
(The boy ran until he lost his breath.)

briah-patch
(BRI-AH-patch) *n.* briar patch; a thick patch of thorny bushes
"Buh Fox t'row Buh Rabbit een de briah-patch."
(Brother Fox threw Brother Rabbit in the thorny bushes.)

brile
(BRILE) *v.* broil/-s/-ed/-ing
"Brile de chickin fuh suppuh."
(Broil the chicken for supper.)

briluh
 (BRIL-uh) *n.* broiler/-s; a small chicken
 "Ma buy uh briluh fuh dinnuh."
 (Mother bought a small chicken for dinner.)

bruk
 (BRUK) *v.* break/-s, broke, breaking
 "Ma drap de cup en' 'e bruk."
 (Mother dropped the cup and it broke.)

bruk
 (BRUK) *adj.* broken
 "De waggin w'eel bruk."
 (The wagon wheel is broken.)

bruk groun'
 (BRUK groun) *v.* break/-s, broke, breaking ground; plow/-s/-ed/-ing
 "Pa gone fiel' fuh bruk-groun'."
 (Father went to plow the field.)

bruk-up
 (BRUK-up) *v.* break/-s, broke, breaking up; finish/-es/-ed/-ing
 "De chu'ch saa'bis done bruk-up."
 (The church service is finished.)

bruro
 (BRU-ro) *n.* bureau/-s
 "Pit de bruro een de bedroom."
 (Put the bureau in the bedroom.)

bubbuh
 (BUB-buh) *n.* brother/-s
 "Bubbuh gimme ten cent."
 (Brother gave me ten cents.)

buck
 (BUCK) *n.* a strong young man
 "'E tek uh buck fuh lif'um."
 (It takes a strong young man to lift it.)

buckruh
 (BUCK-ruh) *n.* white person/-s
 "Me grum'puh wu'k fuh de buckruh."
 (My grandfather worked for the white people.)

bucktoot'
 (BUCK-toot) *adj.* bucktoothed; having front teeth that protrude
 "Dat oagly, bucktoot' gal been duh de paa'ty."
 (That ugly, bucktoothed girl was at the party.)

bu'd
 (bud) *n.* bird/-s
 "Dem shoot fo'teen bu'd."
 (They shoot fourteen birds.)

bugguh-man
 (BUG-GUH-man) *n.* bogyman, bogymen
 "De chillun f'aid de bugguh-man."
 (The children are afraid of the bogyman.)

buh
    (BUH) *n.* brother/s
    "Buh Joe hice de chune."
    (Brother Joe began the song.)

buhniluh
    (buh-NIL-uh) *n.* vanilla
    "Pit uh leetle spoon ub buhniluh een de cake fuh flabuhr'um."
    (Put a teaspoon of vanilla in the cake to give it flavor.)

bull-yellin'
    (bull-YELL-in) *n.* bull yearling; a bull, one to two years old
    "Two bull-yellin' bin tuh de pastuh."
    (There were two young bulls in the pasture.)

bumbo
    (BUM-bo) *n.* the rump
    "Anch 'ting de baby bumbo."
    (Ants stung the baby on his rump.)

bu'n
    (BUN) *v.* burn/-s/-ed/-ing
    "Mus' don' bu'n de toas'."
    (Don't burn the toast.)

bunch-up
    (BUNCH-up) *v.* gather/-s/-ed/-ing
    "'Nuf people bunch-up tuh de po'ch."
    (Many people gathered on the porch.)

bu's'
    (BUS) *v.* burst/-s/-ing
    "De pipe bu's'."
    (The pipe burst.)

'buse
    (BUSE) *v.* abuse/-s/-d, abusing
    "Dat man 'buse 'e lawfully lady."
    (That man abuses his wife.)

'buse'um fuh who las' de longis'
    (BUSE-um fuh who LAS de LONG is) *id.* fight to the finish
    "Jake lef' Jimbo tuh de sto' attuh 'e done 'buse'um fuh who las' de longis'."
    (Jake left Jimbo at the store after they finished fighting.)

bush-chile
    (BUSH-chile) *n.* a child born out of wedlock
    "Dat gal hab uh bush-chile."
    (That girl has an illegitimate child.)

bus' lan'
    (BUS lan) *v.* [bust land]; plow/-s/-ed/-ing
    "Pa gone fiel' fuh bus' lan'."
    (Father went to plow the field.)
    NOTE: *BUS' LAN* AND *BRUK GROUN'* ARE USED INTERCHANGEABLY.

bus' loose
    (bus LOOSE) *v.* bust loose; escape/-s/-d, escaping
    "De mule bus' loose en' gone."
    (The mule freed himself and left.)

bus' out
   (BUS out) *v.* bust out; react in an inappropriate and loud manner
   "De 'ooman bus' out wid de laugh."
   (The women broke into laughter.)

buzzum
   (BUZZ-um) *n.* bosom/-s
   "De maamy hol' de sick chile tuh 'e buzzum."
   (The mother held the sick child to her bosom.)

buzzut
   (BUZZ-ut) *n.* buzzard/-s
   "'E black same lukkuh buzzut."
   (He is black like a buzzard.)

Buzzut Lope
   (BUZZ-ut LOPE) *PN.* Buzzard Lope; a dance
   "Dem gal duh dance de Buzzut Lope."
   (Those girls are dancing the Buzzard Lope.)

C

cabbadge
   (CAB-badge) *n.* cabbage
   "Uh gone fiel' fuh cut cabbadge."
   (I went to the field to cut cabbage.)

cab'nit
   (CAB-nit) *n.* cabinet/-s
   "Uh pit de bittle een de cab'nit."
   (I put the food in the cabinet.)

cackulate
   (CACK-u-late) *v.* calculate/-s/-d, calculating
   "Uh cackulate dey gwi' git't'ru 'fo' daa'k."
   (I calculate that they will get through before dark.)

'cajun
   (CA-jun) *n.* occasion/-s
   "Uh yent hab 'cajun fuh meet'um."
   (I haven't had the occasion to meet them.)

call 'ese'f
   (CALL e-sef) *v.* call himself/herself; pretend
   "Dat leetle gal call 'ese'f duh cook."
   (That little girl is pretending to cook.)

callrico
   (CALL-ri-co) *n.* calico
   "De ap'un mek ub callrico clawt'."
   (The apron is made of calico.)

call'um out 'e name
   (CALL-UM out e NAME) *id.* to curse someone; to call him/her/them an improper name
   "Ma so bex wid de cat, 'e call'um out 'e name."
   (Mother was so vexed with the cat, she cursed him.)

candl' light'n'
(CAN-DL light-'n) *n.* dusk
"Dem ent knock off 'tell cand'l light'n'."
(They didn't knock off work until dusk.)
NOTE: SEE ALSO *DUS'*, *FUS' DAA'K*, AND *SUN-LEAN FUH DOWN*.

cannibel
(CANN-i-BEL) *n.* cannibal/-s
"Grum'puh tell we cannibel bin tuh Aff'iky."
(Grandfather told us there were cannibals in Africa.)

c'arricktuh
(car-RICK-tuh) *n.* character; reputation/-s
"'E c'arricktuh stan' berry good."
(She has a good reputation.)

c'arricktuh spile
(car-RICK-tuh SPILE) *id.* [his/her] character is/was spoiled
"Jim t'ief de 'ooman chickin, en' 'e c'arricktuh spile."
(Jim stole the woman's chicken, and his character was spoiled.)

case quawtuh
(case QUAWT-uh) *n.* a quarter; a twenty-five-cent coin
"Oonuh please kin gimme uh case quawtuh fuh dese coin?"
(Can you please give me a quarter for these coins?)

'cawch
(CAWCH) *v.* scorch/-es/-ed/-ing
"De 'ooman 'cawch de shu't."
(The woman scorched the shirt.)
NOTE: THE LETTER "S" IS DROPPED AT THE BEGINNING OF HARD CONSONANT COMBINATIONS *SC*, *SP*, AND *SK*.

cawn
(CAWN) *n.* corn
"Crow nyam me cawn."
(Crows ate my corn.)

cawncake
(CAWN-cake) *n.* cornbread
"Ma mek cawncake fuh suppuh."
(Mother made cornbread for supper.)

cawnfiel'
(CAWN-fiel) *n.* cornfield/-s
"De gal, dem, gone wu'k duh de cawnfiel'."
(The girl and the others went to work in the cornfield.)
NOTE: THE EXPRESSION *DEM* INDICATES THAT THERE WERE OTHERS WITH THE GIRL.

cawnhom'ny
(CAWN-hom-ny) *n.* hominy
"Ma cook cawnhom'ny fuh gone 'long de chillun bakin en' aig."
(Mother cooked hominy for the children to eat with their bacon and eggs.)

cawnuh
(CAWN-uh) *n.* corner/-s
"De hog dey dey duh de fench cawnuh."
(The hog is right there in the corner of the fence.)
NOTE: THE WORD *DEY* IS REPEATED TO SHOW THE EXACT SPOT.

cawpse
(CAWPSE) *n.* corpse; coffin/-s
"De mens tote de cawpse tuh de grabeyaa'd."
(The men carried the coffin to the graveyard.)

cawsett
(caw-SETT) *n.* corset/-s
"Ma weh uh cawsett onduhneet' 'e shu't."
(Mother wore a corset under her shirt.)

'ceibe
(CEIBE) *v.* deceive/-s/-d, deceiving
"Dat man 'ceibe 'e lawfully lady."
(That man deceived his wife.)

'ceitful
(CEIT-ful) *adj.* deceitful
"'E too 'ceitful."
(He is very deceitful.)

'cep'
(CEP) *v.* accept/-s/-ed/-ing
"Liza 'cep' de imbrickashun."
(Liza accepted the invitation.)

'cep'
(CEP) *prep.* except; with the exception of
"Eb'rybody done gone 'cep' Bubbuh."
(Everybody has already gone except Bubber.)

'cep'm
(CEP-'m) *conj.* unless; but
"Uh gwine 'cep'm 'e wedduh."
(I'm going unless the weather is bad.)
NOTE: *WEDDUH* IS GENERALLY USED TO INDICATE INCLEMENT WEATHER.

chaa'ge
(CHAAGE) *v.* charge/-s/-d, charging; rush violently forward as if in an attack
"De bull chaa'ge de man."
(The bull charged the man.)

Chaa'stun
(CHAA-stun) *PN.* Charleston, South Carolina
"Bubbuh wu'k tuh Chaa'stun."
(Bubber works in Charleston.)

chany
(CHAN-y) *n.* china tableware
"Nyuse de chany fuh set de table."
(Use the china to set the table.)

Chanyberry
(CHAN-Y-ber-ry) *PN.* Chinaberry tree
"Pa duh res' 'neet' de Chanyberry."
(Father is resting under the Chinaberry tree.)

chaw
(CHAW) *v.* chew/-s/-ed/-ing
"De cow duh chaw 'e cud."
(The cow is chewing her cud.)

cheap'um
(CHEAP-um) *v.* insult/-s/-ed/-ing him/her/it/them
"'E lawfully lady cheap'um."
(His wife insulted him.)

cheer
(CHEER) *n.* chair/-s
"Uh gwi' set een de rockuh cheer."
(I'm going to sit in the rocking chair.)

ches'nott
(ches-NOTT) *n.* chestnut/-s
"De chillun roas' de ches'nott."
(The children roasted the chestnuts.)

chickin
(CHICK-in) *n.* chicken/-s
"Daa'tuh cook two chickin fuh dinnuh."
(Daughter cooked two chickens for dinner.)

chigguh
(CHIG-guh) n. chigger
"De chile duh cry 'kase de chigguh bite 'e meat."
(The child is crying because chiggers are biting him.)

chile
(CHILE) *n.* child
"De chile duh sleep."
(The child is sleeping.)

chillun
(CHIL-lun) *n.* children
"De chillun duh sleep."
(The children are sleeping.)

chillun bakin en' aig
(CHIL-lun bak-in en AIG) *n.* a dish served to children—scrambled egg and crumbled bacon stirred into cooked grits
"Gib Grumma some de chillun bakin en' aig."
(Give Grandmother some of the children's bacon and egg dish.)

chillun gal
(CHIL-lun GAL) *n.* a young girl
"Uh chillun gal min' de baby."
(A young girl tended the baby.)
NOTE: *GAL CHILLUN* REFERS TO TWO OR MORE YOUNG GIRLS. BOYS ARE REFERRED TO AS *MAN CHILLUN*. ONE BOY IS CALLED A *MAN CHILE*.

chillun money
(CHIL-lun MON-ey) *n.* child's fare; half-fare
"Ma pay chillun money fuh Joe ride de strain."
(Mother paid half-fare for Joe to ride the train.)

chimbly
(CHIM-bly) *n.* chimney/-s; fireplace
"Sandy Claw come down de chimbly."
(Santa Claus came down the chimney.)

chinkypen
(chink-y-PEN) *n.* chinquapin/-s
"Dem duh gedduh chinkypen."
(They are gathering chinquapins.)

chit'l'n'
(CHIT-l'n) *n.* chitterling/-s
"Chit'l'n' stan' berry good 'long cawnbread."
(Chitterlings are very good with cornbread.)

chu'ch
(CHUCH) *n.* church/-es
"Saint Mikul Chu'ch dey tuh Broad Skreet een Chaa'stun."
(Saint Michael's Church is there on Broad Street in Charleston.)

chu'chyaa'd
(chuch-YAAD) *n.* churchyard/-s
"De blessit dead sleep een de chu'chyaa'd."
(The blessed dead sleep in the churchyard.)

Chuseday
(CHUSE-day) *PN.* Tuesday
"Ef 'e is marri'd, 'e gwi' marri'd Chuseday."
(If she does get married, she will be married on Tuesday.)

chune
(CHUNE) *n.* tune/-s; song/-s
"Buh Joe hice de chune."
(Brother Joe began the song.)

chunk
(CHUNK) *v.* throw
"Chunk de trash een de fiah."
(Throw de trash in the fire.)

chunk-up
(CHUNK-up) *v.* stoke; tend, as a fire
"Chunk-up de fiah fuh bile de watuh."
(Add wood to the fire so the water will boil.)

chupit
(CHU-pit) *adj.* stupid
"De chillun mek fiah 'neet' de house, dem dat chupit."
(The children are so stupid they made a fire under the house.)
NOTE: USE OF THE WORD *DAT* INDICATES DEGREE. IN THIS CASE, THE CHILDREN WERE *VERY* STUPID.

cibul
(CI-bul) *adj.* civil
"Joe tek'um tuh cibul co't."
(Joe took them to civil court.)

cinduh
(CIN-duh) *n.* cinder/-s; ashes
"Cinduh mek good paa't."
(Cinders make a good path.)

cin'mum
(CIN-mum) *n.* cinnamon
"Pit some cin'mum een de pie."
(Put some cinnamon in the pie.)

cistun
(CIS-tun) *n.* cistern/-s; water tank/-s

"De cistun dry."
(There is no water in the cistern.)

citify
(CIT-i-fy) *adj.* citified
"Dat gal citify, enty?"
(That girl is citified, isn't she?)

cla' tuh Gawd
(cla tuh GAWD) *interj.* I declare to God!
"Cla' tuh Gawd Uh ent shum!"
(I declare to God I didn't see him.)

clabbuh-claw
(CLAB-buh-CLAW) *v.* [clobber claw]; maul/-s/-ed/-ing; beat/-s/-ing
"De gal clabbuh-claw de boy good-fashi'n."
(The girl beat the boy thoroughly.)

clap-hat-bitch
(CLAP-hat-BITCH) *n.* a shrewish, bullying woman; a virago
"Dat clap-hat-bitch done clabbuh-claw 'e juntlemun, clap 'e hat on 'e head, en' gone."
(That virago has mauled her husband, put on her hat, and left.)

clawt'
(CLAWT) *n.* cloth
"Daa'tuh buy t'ree yaa'd ub clawt'."
(Daughter bought three yards of cloth.)

climb de ecknowledge tree
(CLIMB de ECK-now-ledge tree) *id.* become educated
"De chillun gone school fuh climb de ecknowledge tree."
(The children went to school to become educated.)

clumpsy
(KLUMP-sy) *adj.* clumsy
"Della fall een de ditch; 'e dat clumpsy."
(Della fell in the ditch; she is that clumsy.)

'coat
(COAT) *n.* petticoat/-s
"Dat clawt' stan' berry good fuh mek 'coat."
(That cloth is very good to use in making a petticoat.)

cock 'e yez
(COCK e yez) *v.* cock his/her/its ears; listen carefully
"'E cock 'e yez fuh yeddy'um."
(She cocked her ears to hear them.)

col'
(COL) *n.* cold
"'E hab hebby col'."
(He has a severe cold.)

col'
(COL) *adj.* cold
"De chile foot col'."
(The child's feet are cold.)

col' hom'ny 'ooman
(COL hom-ny OO-MAN *id.* a worthless, inconsiderate

woman
"Della bin uh col' hom'ny 'ooman."
(Della was a worthless woman.)
NOTE: THE REFERENCE TO COLD HOMINY INDICATES THAT THE WOMAN IS SO INCONSIDERATE SHE GIVES HER FAMILY COLD HOMINY TO EAT.

colluh
(COL-luh) *n.* collar/-s
"De colluh du'tty."
(The collar is dirty.)

colluh
(COL-luh) *n.* color/-s
"Wuh colluh 'e yiz?"
(What color is it?)

coob
(COOB) *n.* coop/-s
"Twelbe hen bin een de coob."
(Twelve hens were in the coop.)

cootuh
(COOT-uh) *n.* cooter/-s; turtle/-s
"Cootuh good fuh mek soup."
(Cooters make good soup.)

coppuhratuh
(cop-puh-RAT-uh) *n.* carburetor/-s
"De cyaa' coppuhratuh ent specify."
(The carburetor on the car is not working.)

cos'
(COS) *v.* cost/-s/-ing
"De han' t'read cos' fibe cent."
(The thread cost five cents.)

co'se
(COSE) *n.* course/-s
"De ribbuh co'se tu'n tuh Maa'tun P'int."
(The course of the river changes at Martin's Point.)

co'se
(COSE) *adj.* coarse
"De clawt' bin too co'se fuh mek de dress."
(The cloth was too coarse to make the dress.)

'co'se
(COSE) *conj.* of course
"'Co'se Uh gwine."
(Of course I'm going.)

co't
(COT) *n.* court/-s
"De 'ooman tek'um tuh co't."
(The woman took them to court.)

co't
(COT) *v.* court/-s/-ed/-ing
"Jeems bin co't de gal since Augus' munt'."
(James has been courting the girl since August.)

co'thouse
(COT-house) *n.* courthouse/-s
"All de mens gone tuh de co'thouse."
(All the men have gone to the courthouse.)

could'uh
 (COULD-uh) v. could have
 "Ef 'e lef' mo'soonuh, 'e could'uh ketch de strain."
 (If he had left sooner, he could have caught the train.)

cowcumbuh
 (COW-cum-BUH) n. cucumber/-s
 "Cowcumbuh done come een."
 (Cucumbers are ready to be harvested.)

cow-paa't
 (COW-paat) n. cow path/-s; a narrow path generally made by animals traveling the same track repeatedly
 "Dem folluh de cow-paa't 'long de ribbuhbank."
 (They followed the cow path along the riverbank.)

crack 'e teet'
 (CRACK e TEET) v. crack his/her teeth; speak
 "Ma ent crack 'e teet'."
 (Mother did not say anything.)

crap
 (CRAP) n. crop/-s
 "De crap done ready fuh haa'bis."
 (The crop is ready to be harvested.)

'crape
 (CRAPE) v. scrape/-s/-d/-ing
 "De boy 'crape 'e foot on de oshtuh shell."
 (The boy scraped his foot on the oyster shell.)

credenshul
 (CRE-den-shul) n. credential/-s; valuable possessions
 "Ma keep 'e credenshul een 'e trunk."
 (Mother keeps her valuable possessions in her trunk.)

credik
 (CRED-ik) v. credit/-s/-ed/-ing; charge/-s/-ed/-ing
 "Uh ent able fuh credik de g'ocery."
 (I wasn't able to charge the groceries.)

creetuh
 (CREE-tuh) n. creature/-s
 "De po' creetuh 'mos' staa'b tuh de't'."
 (The poor creature is nearly starved to death.)

crick
 (CRICK) n. creek/-s
 "W'en 'e col' duh wintuhtime, Uh gone duh crick fuh grain."
 (When it was cold in the wintertime, I went to the creek to spear fish.)

cronch
 (CRONCH) v. crunch; break/-s, broke, breaking
 "Cronch de toas' een de soup."
 (Break up the toast in the soup.)
 NOTE: THE WORD *CRONCH* IS USED TO IMITATE THE SOUND OF TOAST BREAKING. ONOMATOPOEIA IS FREQUENTLY FOUND IN GULLAH.

crookety
(CROOK-e-ty) *adj.* crooked
"De chimbly stan' sawtuh crookety."
(The chimney looks a little crooked.)

cross obuh
(CROSS obuh) *v.* [cross over]; die/-s/-d, dying
"Maum Beck cross obuh de two Sat'd'y done gone."
(Ma Beck died Saturday two weeks ago.)

cross road sto'
(CROSS road STO) *n.* a store located where two or more roads cross
"Gally gone cross road sto' fuh 'e git payoff."
(Gally went to the crossroad store to be paid her wages.)
NOTE: THE CROSSROAD STORE WAS A COMMON MEETING PLACE IN THE 1920s. CROSSROAD IS WRITTEN AS TWO WORDS TO SHOW THAT EQUAL STRESS IS PLACED ON EACH WHEN SPOKEN.

crotch
(CROTCH) *n.* crutch/-es
"'E nyuse crotch 'kase 'e foot bruk."
(He uses crutches because his foot is broken.)

crutch
(CRUTCH) *n.* crotch/-es
"De coon dey dey een de crutch ub de tree."
(The raccoon is right there in the crotch of the tree.)

cubo'd
(CUB-od) *n.* cupboard/-s
"Pit de dish een de cubo'd."
(Put the dishes in the cupboard.)

cu'leh'we'go
(CU-leh-we-GO) *id.* come let us go
"Cu'leh'we'go home!"
(Come, let us go home!)

cum'fuh'shum
(CUM-fuh-SHUM) *id.* come/came to see him/her/them
"Dem cum'fuh'shum."
(They came to see him.)

cump'ny
(CUMP-ny) *n.* company; companionship
"Uh glad fuh hab dey cump'ny."
(I'm glad to have their company.)

'cump'ny
(CUMP-ny) *v.* accompany, -ied, -ied, -ing
"Me niece 'cump'ny'um tuh towng."
(My niece accompanied them to town.)

cumpuhsary
(cum-puh-SAR-y) *n.* commissary, commissaries
"Dem gone cumpuhsary fuh buy bittle."
(They went to the commissary to buy food.)
NOTE: THIS WORD BE HEARD TODAY ONLY ON MILITARY BASES.

Virginia Mixson Geraty

IN THE PAST, COMMISSARIES WERE SET UP ON PLANTATIONS.

cumpuhsayshun
(CUM-puh-SAY-shun) *n.* conversation/-s
"'E hol' cumpuhsayshun 'long'um."
(She held a conversation with him.)

cunjuh
(CUN-juh) *n.* conjure; an object made by someone who practices witchcraft
"De cunjuh t'row spell 'pun de gal."
(The conjure cast a spell on the girl.)

cunnel
(cun-NEL) *n.* canal/-s
"Dey ketch de 'gatuh duh de cunnel."
(They caught the alligator in the canal.)

cunny
(CUN-ny) *adj.* cunning
"Buh Rabbit too cunny."
(Brother Rabbit is very cunning.)

cuntrady
(cun-TRAD-Y) *adj.* contrary
"De ole mule lazy en' cuntrady alltwo."
(That old mule is both lazy and contrary.)

cunweenyunt
(cun-WEEN-yunt) *n.* convenience
"Pa 'pen'pun 'e mule fuh 'e cunweenyunt."
(Father depends on his mule for convenience. The mule carries him about.)

cunwince
(cun-WINCE) *v.* convince/-s/-ed/-ing
"Fin'lly at las' Ma cunwince Bubbuh fuh gone."
(At last Mother convinced Brother to go.)

curlyflowuh
(CUR-ly-flow-uh) *n.* cauliflower
"Dey plant tomatuh en' curlyflowuh."
(They planted tomatoes and cauliflower.)

'cuse
(CUSE) *v.* accuse/-s/-d, accusing
"'E 'cuse'um duh t'ief de hog."
(He accused him of stealing the hog.)

cuss'um 'neet 'e clothes
(CUSS-um neet e CLOTHES) *id.* curse someone by calling them an ass, a part of the human body that is usually clothed
"De gal dat bex 'e cuss'um 'neet' 'e clothes."
(The girl was so vexed she called him an ass.)

cut de pidgin wing
(CUT de PID-gin wing) *v.*

dance the Pigeon Wing
"Buh Joe beat stick fuh de
chillun cut de pidgin wing."
(Brother Joe beat sticks
together to keep time for the
children to dance the Pigeon
Wing.)

cu'tesy
(CUT-e-sy) *adj.* courteous
"Dem gal berry cu'tesy."
(Those girls are very courteous.)

cut 'e yeye
(CUT e YEYE) *v.* cut his/her
eye; glance from the corner
of the eye, indicating
suspicion or contempt
"De chile bin play duh chu'ch
'tell 'e Ma cut 'e yeye at
um."
(The child was playing in
church until his mother cut
her eye at him.)

cut-out
(CUT-out) v. leave immediately
"W'en 'e yeddy de bell, 'e
cut-out."
(When the bell rang, he left
immediately.)

cut'um down
(CUT-um DOWN) *v.* cut him/
her/them down; insult/-s/-ed/
-ing him/her/them
"'Lizabet' cut'um down 'tell 'e
yeye duh leak."
(Elizabeth insulted her until
she cried.)

cya'
(CYA) *v.* carry, carries,
carried, carrying
"Us cya' de chile tuh 'e ma."
(We carried the child to his
mother.)

cyaa'
(CYAA) *n.* car/-s
"Us cya'um een de cyaa'."
(We carried him in the car.)

cyaa'b
(CYAAB) *v.* carve/-s/-d,
carving
"Ma show'um how fuh cyaa'b
de tuckrey."
(Mother showed them how to
carve the turkey.)

cyaa'd
(CYAAD) *n.* card/-s
"Dem play cyaa'd 'tell
middlenight."
(They played cards until
midnight.)

cyaaf
(CYAAF) *n.* calf, calves
"De cow hab cyaaf 'fo'
dayclean."
(The cow had the calf before
sunrise.)

cyaa'idge
(CYAA-idge) *n.* carriage/-s
"Dat hawss ent lub fuh pull
cyaa'idge."
(That horse doesn't like to pull
a carriage.)

cyaam
(CYAAM) *adj.* calm

"De watuh cyaam; us gwi'
    cas' de net."
(The water is calm; we're
    going to cast the net.)

cyaa'pentuh
(CYAA-pen-tuh) *n.* carpenter/-s
"De cyaa'pentuh cum'fuh bil'
    de baa'n."
(The carpenter has come to
    build the barn.)

cyaa't
(CYAAT) *n.* cart/-s
"De cyaa't w'eel bruk."
(The cart wheel is broken.)

cyackly
(CYACK-ly) *v.* cackle/-s/-ed/
    -ing
"De hen cyackly w'en 'e done
    fuh lay."
(The hen cackles when she has
    finished laying.)

cyan'
(CYAN) *v.* can't
"De leetle gal cyan' tote de
    baby."
(The little girl can't carry the
    baby.)

cyan' done
(CYAN done) *adv.* extremely;
    without end
"Dat 'ooman oagly cyan'
    done."
(That woman is extremely
    ugly. There is no end to her
    ugliness.)

cyan' specify
(CYAN spec-i-fy) *adj.* useless;
    unsatisfactory
"De cyaa't cyan' specify; de
    w'eel bruk."
(The cart is useless; the wheel
    is broken.)

cyas'
(CYAS) *v.* cast/-s/-ing
"De Lawd cyas' Mistuh Adam
    en' Miss Ebe out de
    gyaa'd'n."
(The Lord cast Mister Adam
    and Miss Eve out of the
    garden.)

cyaskut
(CYAS-kut) *n.* casket/-s
"Uh putty reef bin 'pun'top de
    cyaskut."
(There was a pretty wreath on
    top of the casket.)

cyas' net
(CYAS net) *n.* cast net/-s
"Bubbuh ketch 'nuf swimp een
    'e cyas' net."
(Brother caught many shrimp
    in his cast net.)

cyo'
(CYO) *v.* cure/-s/-ed/-ing
"Ma g'em elbo' soda fuh cyo'
    'e mis'ry."
(Mother gave him bicarbonate
    of soda to cure his discom-
    fort.)
NOTE: *ELBO' SODA* WAS SO
NAMED BECAUSE OF THE ILLUS-
TRATION ON THE ARM AND
HAMMER BAKING SODA BOX.

D

da' wuh mek'um stan' so
(DA wuh mek-um STAN so) *id.* that is why it is the way it is; that is why it looks the way it does
"Saint Mikul bil'um. Da' wuh mek'um stan' so."
(Saint Michael built it. That's why it looks the way it does.)
NOTE: THE REFERENCE HERE IS TO ST. MICHAEL'S CHURCH IN CHARLESTON, SOUTH CAROLINA, AND THE BELIEF EXPRESSED BY A FLOWER LADY THAT ST. MICHAEL BUILT THE CHURCH.

daa'tuh
(DAA-tuh) *n.* daughter/-s
"Daa'tuh gone sto'."
(Daughter went to the store.)

dainjus
(DAIN-jus) *adj.* dangerous
"Dat leetle bull-yellin' berry dainjus."
(That little yearling bull is very dangerous.)

dan
(DAN) *conj.* than
"'E mo' tall dan me."
(He is taller than I.)

dance-man
(DANCE-man) *n.* a professional male dancer
"T'ree dance-man bin duh de sukkus."
(There were three professional dancing men in the circus.)

dat
(DAT) *adj.* that
"Dat hat de gal own."
(That is the girl's hat.)

dat
(DAT) *adv.* that
"Dem nyam dry cawnhom'ny; dem dat hongry."
(They ate plain corn hominy; they were that hungry.)
NOTE: DAT USED WITH ANOTHER ADVERB OR ADJECTIVE EXPRESSES SUPERLATIVE DEGREE.

dayclean
(day-CLEAN) *n.* sunrise; daylight; dawn; daybreak
"Dayclean uh gone wu'k."
(At sunrise I went to work.)

de
(DE) *adj.* the
"De cat dead."
(The cat is dead.)

dead man finguh
(DEAD man FIN-guh) *n.* dead-man's-fingers; one of the inedible organs of a crab
"Mus' don' nyam de dead man finguh."
(You must not eat the dead-man's-fingers.)

Debble
(DEB-ble) *PN.* Devil
"De Debble mek'um t'ief."
(The Devil made them steal.)

debblement
(deb-ble-MENT) *n.* devilment; mischief

"Debblement weh dat chile
  lib."
(Mischief is all that child
  thinks about.)

debble ub uh t'ing
(DEB ble ub uh TING) *n.*
  devil of a thing; a trying
  situation
"Dishyuh uh debble ub uh
  t'ing."
(This here is a devil of a
  thing.)

deef
(DEEF) *adj.* deaf
"De ole man bline en' deef
  alltwo."
(The old man is both blind and
  deaf.)

deestruss
(DEE-strus) *adj.* distressed;
  worried
"Sistuh eye duh leak, 'e dat
  deestrus'."
(Sister is crying, she is so
  distressed.)

deestunt
(DEE-stunt) *adv.* decently;
  properly
"Ma tell me ef uh yent ack
  deestunt uh cyan' gone
  chu'ch."
(Mother told me if I didn't act
  properly I couldn't go to
  church.)

dem
(DEM) *pron.* they/them;
  others
"Jake, dem, gone to towng."
(Jake and the others went to
  town.)

dem'own
(DEM-own) *pron.* their own;
  their/-s
"De cyaa't dem'own."
(The cart belongs to them.)

demse'f
(dem-SEF) *pron.* themselves
"Dey done'um demse'f."
(They did it themselves.)

Demmycrack
(DEM-my-crack) *PN.* Democrat/-s
"Buh Joe tell we 'e binnuh
  Demmycrack."
(Brother Joe told us he was a
  Democrat.)

den
(DEN) *adv.* then
"W'en 'e fus' daa'k, den Uh
  gwine."
(When it is dusk, then I'm
  going.)

des'
(DES) *adv.* just; recently
"'E des' moobe yuh."
(He just moved here.)

dese
(DESE) *pron.* these
"Dese Ma chickin."
(These are Mother's chickens.)

deseyuh
(dese-YUH) *id.* these [here]
"Deseyuh chickin me own."
(These chickens here are mine.)

de't' shet out 'e light
(DET shet out e LIGHT) *id.*
death shut out his/her/its light; he/she/it died
"'E wu'k eb'ry day 'tell de't shet out 'e light."
(He worked every day until he died.)

dey
(DEY) *pron.* they
"Dey wu'k 'long'um."
(They worked along with him.)

dey
(DEY) *adv.* there
"Dem bin dey yistiddy."
(They were there yesterday.)

dey dey
(DEY DEY) *id.* right there
"Dem bin dey dey 'fo' dayclean."
(They were right there before sunrise.)

deyfo'
(DEY-fo) *adv.* therefore; for that reason
"Uh yent know 'bout'um, deyfo' Uh yent gwi' crack me teet'!"
(I don't know about it, therefore I'm not going to say anything.)

dibe
(DIBE) *v.* dive
"Uh try fuh ketch de cootuh 'fo' 'e dibe 'neet' de watuh."
(I tried to catch the cooter before he dived under the water.)

diff'unce
(DIFF-unce) *n.* difference/-s
"Dey ent dat much diff'unce 'tween de two gal."
(There isn't that much difference between the two girls.)

dig du't
(dig DUT) *v.* run/ran so fast the feet dig up dirt
"'E dig du't down de road."
(He ran so fast down the road his feet were digging up dirt.)

dignify
(dig-ni-FY) *adv.* with dignity; gracefully
"Miss 'Lizabet' dance berry dignify."
(Miss Elizabeth dances very gracefully.)

dinnuh
(DIN-nuh) *n.* dinner
"Dem nyam 'tettuh fuh dinnuh."
(They ate potatoes for dinner.)

dis
(DIS) *pron.* this
"Dis de man wuh t'ief de hog."
(This is the man who stole the hog.)

disapp'int
(dis-ap-PINT) *adj.* disappointed
"De gal bin berry disapp'int w'en de strain lef'um."
(The girl was very disappointed when the train left her.)

disgus'
(dis-GUS) *adj.* disgusted
"Pa bin disgus' w'en de wurrum nyam 'e crap."
(Father was disgusted when the worms ate his crop.)

dishyuh
(dish-YUH) *id.* this [here]
"Dishyuh de bes' cake."
(This one here is the best cake.)

disso
(DIS-so) *adv.* just so; for no particular reason
"Uh come 'long disso."
(I came along for no particular reason.)

distrackit meet'n'
(DIS-track-it MEET-'n) *id.* a protracted prayer meeting
"T'ree pastuh speak tuh de distrackit meet'n'."
(Three pastors spoke at the protracted prayer meeting.)

distruss
(dis-TRUSS) *adj.* distressed
"Willie distruss bekase 'e boat done racktify 'long de harricane."
(Willie is distressed because his boat was destroyed in the hurricane.)

do'
(DOH) *n.* door/-s
"Shet de do'."
(Shut the door.)

'do'
(DOH) *conj.* although
'Do' 'e strong, 'e cyan' specify fuh do'um."
(Although he is strong, he isn't able to do it.)

dolluh
(DOL-luh) *n.* dollar/-s
"De shoesh cos' fibe dolluh."
(The shoes cost five dollars.)

domineckuh hen
(dom-i-NECK-uh) *n.* a Dominique chicken
"Ma domineckuh hen hab fo' biddy."
(Mother's Dominique hen has four biddies.)

don'
(DOHN) *v.* do not
"Don' gone duh crick."
(Do not go in the creek.)

done
(DUN) *adv.* used with action verbs to show past tense
"'E suh 'e yent done cook de dinnuh."
(She says she hasn't finished cooking the dinnuh.)

done fuh
(DUN fuh) *id.* is completely
"Dat gal done fuh lazy."
(That girl is extremely lazy.)

do'um
(DO-um) *id.* do/does/did/doing it/them
"W'en oonuh gwi' do'um?"
(When are you going to do it?)

don' fly een Gawd face
(don FLY een GAWD face) *id.*
[don't fly in God's face];
accept God's will submissively
"Mus' don' mek hebby complain; don' fly een Gawd face!"
(Do not protest; accept God's will!)

do'um bad
(do-um BAD) *v.* mistreat
"De 'ooman juntlemun do'um bad."
(The woman's husband mistreated her.)

down tuh de salt
(DOWN tuh de SALT) *id.*
down to the ocean
"Dem gone down tuh de salt fuh fish."
(They went down to the sea to fish.)

drag 'e foot
(DRAG e FOOT) *id.* walk very slowly; waste time
"Mek oonuh duh drag 'e foot?"
(Why are you walking so slowly?)

drap
(DRAP) *v.* drop/-s, dropped, dropping
"De butluh drap de chany."
(The butler dropped the china.)

drap een
(DRAP een) *id.* drop in; visit/-s/-ed/-ing
"Sistuh drap een teday."
(Sister visited today.)

drap 'roun'
(drap ROUN) *id.* drop around; visit/-s/-ed/-ing
"Mek oonuh ent drap 'roun' Sunday?"
(Why didn't you visit Sunday?)

drap sleep
(drap SLEEP) *id.* drop to sleep; go to sleep
"Pa drap sleep duh chu'ch."
(Father went to sleep in church.)

drap uh cutchy
(DRAP uh CUTCH-y) *v.* [drop a] curtsy; bow/-s/-ed/-ing
"De leetle gal drap uh cutchy."
(The little girl bowed.)

dreen
(DREEN) *n.* drain/-s
"De dreen jam up."
(The drain is blocked.)

dreen
(DREEN) *v.* drain/-s/-ed/-ing
"Dreen de watuh off de gritch."
(Drain the water off the grits.)

dribe
(DRIBE) *v.* drive/-s, drove, driving
"Dribe de chickin out de gyaa'd'n."
(Drive the chickens out of the garden.)

dribuh
(DRIB-uh) *n.* driver/-s
"Uh seddown 'longside de dribuh."
(I sat [down] beside the driver.)

drowndid
(DROWN-did) *v.* drown/-s/-ed/-ing
"De rat drowndid een de crick."
(The rat drowned in the creek.)

dry-bone
(DRY-bone) *id.* extremely thin
"De gal dry-bone."
(The girl is extremely thin.)

dry cawnhom'ny
(DRY cawn-hom-ny) *n.* hominy served plain, without butter or gravy
"Dat man so po' 'e haffuh nyam dry cawnhom'ny."
(That man is so poor he has to eat hominy without gravy or butter.)

dry-drought
(DRY-drought) *n.* drought; excessively dry weather
"Dry-drought hab de crap."
(Dry weather has ruined the crop.)

dry 'long so
(dry long SO) *id.* without decoration; pure and simple
"Ma mek de dress dry 'long so."
(Mother made the dress without frills and trimmings.)

dub
(DUB) *n.* dove/-s
"Dem gone fuh hunt dub."
(They went to hunt doves.)

duh
(DUH) *prep.* in, to, on, toward, during, for, of, at
"'E col' duh wintuhtime."
(It is cold during the winter.)

duh
(DUH) *v.* is, are, were, do, does; used in conjunction with an action verb
"Dem duh dance."
(They are dancing.)

duh two time
(duh TWO time) *adv.* twice
"Uh done tell oonuh duh two time mus' lef' dat gal 'lone."
(I have already told you twice to leave that girl alone.)

'dultrify
(DULT-ri-fy) *v.* commit adultery
"De jedge suh de man 'dultrify."
(The judge charged the man with adultery.)

dunkyuh
(DUNK-yuh) *v.* do/does/did not care
"Uh dunkyuh huccome 'e gone."
(I do not care why he left.)

dus'
(DUS) *n.* dusk; twilight

"Dem come home 'fo' dus'."
(They came home before dusk.)
NOTE: SEE ALSO *CANDL' LIGHT'N'*, *FUS' DAA'K*, AND *SUN-LEAN FUH DOWN*.

dus'
(DUS) *n.* dust
"De dus' kibbuh de cheer en' de table."
(The dust covers the chairs and the tables.)

dus'
(DUS) *v.* dust/-s/-ed/-ing
"Nyuse de clawt' fuh dus'um."
(Use the cloth to dust them.)

du't
(DUT) *n.* dirt; earth
"Don' plant de seed too deep een de du't."
(Do not plant the seeds too deep in the earth.)

du'tty
(DUT-ty) *adj.* dirty
"De chile done fuh du'tty"
(The child is extremely dirty.)

E

'e
(E) *pron.* he, she, it
"'E done gone."
(He has already gone.)

Eart'
(EART) *n.* Earth
"Gawd mek de Eart'."
(God made the Earth.)

eart'
(EART) *n.* soil; dirt
"De cawn need good eart' fuh mek."
(The corn needs rich soil to grow well.)

ebbuh
(EBB-uh) *adv.* ever; always
"Dem ebbuh did lib dey dey."
(They always lived right there.)

ebbuhlastin'
(EBB-uh-LAST-in) *adj.* everlasting
"'E drowndid tuh ebbuhlastin' de't'."
(He drowned to everlasting death.)

Ebe
(EBE) *PN.* Eve
"Miss Ebe en' Mistuh Adam lib een de Gyaa'd'n ub Ed'n."
(Miss Eve and Mister Adam lived in the Garden of Eden.)

ebe
(EBE) *n.* eave/-s
"De coon gone 'neet' de ebe."
(The raccoon went under the eaves of the house.)

ebenin'
(EBE-nin) *n.* evening/-s
"Uh gwi' drap 'roun' dis ebenin'."
(I'm going to visit this evening.)

ebenin'
(EBE-nin) *interj.* good evening

"Ebenin', suh!"
(Good evening, sir!)

eb'n
(EB-'n) *adj.* even; straight
"De frock tail ent eb'n.'
(The hem of the dress isn't even.)

eb'n'so
(EB-'n-so) *adv.* even so; although
"Uh ent git eenbite; eb'n'so Uh gwine."
(I didn't get an invitation; even so, I am going.)

eb'ry
(EB-ry) *adj.* every
"Eb'ry Sattyday dem hab paa'ty."
(Every Saturday they have a party.)

eb'rybody
(EB-ry-bod-y) *pron.* everybody
"Eb'rybody 'cep' me, one, hab eenbitation."
(Everybody except me alone has an invitation.)

eb'ryt'ing
(EB-RY-ting) *pron.* everything
"Eb'ryt'ing ready fuh de saa'bis."
(Everything is ready for the service.)

eb'ryweh
(EB-RY-weh) *adv.* everywhere
"Ma saa'ch eb'ryweh fuh 'e shoesh."
(Mother searched everywhere for her shoes.)

ecknowledge
(eck-NOWL-edge) *n.* knowledge; education
"De chillun gone school fuh git ecknowledge."
(The children went to school to get an education.)

eddycashun
(ed-dy-CA-shun) *n.* education
"Dem chillun dey dey ent hab no eddycashun."
(Those children right there don't have any education.)

eeduh
(EE-duh) *adv.* either
"De baby sick eeduh 'e sp'il."
(The baby is either sick or he is spoiled.)

eeduhso
(EE-DUH-so) *adv.* [either so]; or else
"Dem gwi' come fuh wissit, eeduhso Uh gwine fuh shum."
(They are coming for a visit, or else I am going to see them.)

eegnunt
(EEG-nunt) *adj.* ignorant
"'E eegnunt en' 'e haa'dhead alltwo."
(He is both ignorant and stubborn.)

een
(EEN) *prep.* in; inside

"De pastuh gone een de chu'ch."
(The pastor went inside the church.)

eenbite
(een-BITE) *v.* invite/-s/-ed/-ing
"All de chillun eenbite tuh de wedd'n'."
(All the children are invited to the wedding.)

eenbitashun
(EEN-bi-TASH-un) *n.* invitation/-s
"Uh gwi' sen' eenbitashun; oonuh mus' sho' en' dey dey!"
(I'm going to send an invitation; you must be sure to come!)
NOTE: ALSO USED FOR "INVITATION" ARE THE WORDS *EENBITE* AND *IMBRICKASHUN*.

een de fus' gwinin' off
(een de FUS gwin-in off) *id.* in the beginning
"Een de fus' gwinin' off de Lawd mek Mistuh Adam."
(In the beginning the Lord made Mister Adam.)

een 'e shu't-sleebe
(een e SHUT-sleebe) *id.* in his shirt sleeves; without a jacket
"Pa gone ch'ch een 'e shu't-sleebe."
(Father went to church without a jacket.)

een'fol
(een-FOL) *adj.* [in foal]; pregnant
"De gal een'fol."
(The girl is pregnant.)

een he'lt'
(EEN helt) *adj.* [in health]; pregnant
"Alltwo de gal een he'lt'."
(Both the girls are pregnant.)
NOTE: THE WORDS *EEN'FOL* AND *EEN HE'LT'* ARE USED INTERCHANGEABLY.

eenjine
(EEN-jine) *n.* engine/-s
"De eenjine done racktify."
(The engine has been broken for some time.)

eenjurin'
(een-JUR-in) *adv.* during
"Pa bin sleep eenjurin' de meet'n'."
(Father was sleeping during the meeting.)

eenjy
(EEN-jy) *v.* enjoy/-s/-ed/-ing
"All ub we eenjy de sukkus."
(All of us enjoyed the circus.)

eenjy
(EEN-jy) *v.* experience
"Grum'pa duh eenjy berry po' he'lt'. Gramma duh eenjy berry good he'lt'."
(Grandfather is in very poor health. Grandmother is in very good health.)

eensult
(EEN-sult) *v.* insult/-s/-ed/-ing
"Ben eensult'um en' 'e

knock'um."
(Ben insulted her and she hit him.)

eentitlement
(een-TIT-LE-ment) *n.* title; a word used to show a person's rank or position
"Reb'ren' 'e eentitlement."
(Reverend is his title.)

eentuhfayre
(EEN-TUH-fayre) *v.* interfere/-s/-d, interfering
"De Lawd scole Mistuh Saa'punt fuh eentuhfayre wid 'E bidness."
(The Lord scolded Mister Serpent for interfering with His business.)

een uh bad way
(EEN uh BAD way) *id.* in a bad way; very ill
"De ole 'ooman een uh bad way."
(The old woman is very ill.)

eetch
(EETCH) *n.* itch/-es
"'E hab de Seb'n Yeah Eetch."
(She has the Seven Year Itch.)

eetch
(EETCH) *v.* itch/-es/-ed/-ing
"'E han' duh eetch."
(Her hand is itching.)

ef
(EF) *conj.* if
"Uh ax'um ef 'e gwine."
(I asked him if he was going.)

Ef oonuh yent hab hawss fuh ride, ride cow.
(ef oo-nuh yent hab HAWSS fuh ride RIDE cow) *id.* If you don't have a horse to ride, ride a cow. Make the best of the situation.

'e gwi' wedduh
(e gwi WED-DUH) *id.* the weather is going to be bad: rain, wind, etc.
"De chillun gone home 'kase 'e gwi' wedduh."
(The children went home because it is going to rain.)

'e haa't gone een 'e shoesh
(e HAAT gone een e SHOESH) *id.* [his heart is gone in his shoes]; he/she lost his/her courage
"W'en de animel tu'n 'roun', 'e haa't gone een 'e shoesh."
(When the animal turned around, he lost his courage.)

'E jaw teet' full wid lie.
(e JAW teet FULL wid LIE) *id.* His/her jaw teeth are filled with lies. He/she is a liar.

elbo' soda
(EL-bo SO-DA) *n.* baking soda
"Elbo' soda good fuh clean de flo'."
(Baking soda is good for cleaning floors.)
NOTE: "ELBO'" IS TAKEN FROM THE ILLUSTRATION ON THE ARM AND HAMMER BAKING SODA BOX.

else so
(else SO) *conj.* otherwise
"'E mus' gone school, else so 'e Ma gwi' lick'um."
(She must go to school, otherwise her mother is going to punish her.)

ellyment
(EL-LY-ment) *n.* element; the sky
"De bu'd duh fly 'bout een de ellyment."
(The birds are flying about in the sky.)

en'
(EN) *conj.* and
"Ma buy rice en' 'tettuh."
(Mother bought rice and potatoes.)

ent
(ENT) *v.* is/are/do/does/did not
"Dat gal ent gwine 'long'um."
(That girl is not going with them.)
NOTE: *ENT* BECOMES *YENT* WHEN PRECEDED BY A VOWEL.

enty
(ENT-y) *id.* is it not so?
"Oonuh gwine chu'ch, enty?"
(You are going to church, are you not?)

ent wu't'
(ent-WUT) *id.* has no worth
"Dat 'ooman too lazy; 'e ent wu't'."
(That woman is too lazy; she is worthless.)

Epprul
(EPP-rul) *PN.* April
"'E alltime wedduh een Epprul munt'."
(It always rains in April.)

'ese'f
(e-SEF) *pron.* he/she/him/her/itself
"De boy 'ese'f gwine."
(The boy is going himself.)
NOTE: *'ESE'F* AND *'SE'F* ARE USED INTERCHANGEABLY.

'e stan' so
(e STAN so) *id.* it is so; it appears to be so
"Dat wuh 'e stan' so."
(That's why it looks that way.)

'E time fuh gone.
(e time fuh GONE) *id.* It's time to go.

exceed
(EX-ceed) *v.* succeed/-s/-ed/-ing
"'E nebbuh exceed fuh bil' de house."
(He never succeeded in building the house.)

exwance
(EX-wance) *n.* advance/-s
"Bubbuh ax fuh exwance on 'e wage."
(Brother asked for an advance on his wages.)

exwantage
(EX-want-age) *n.* advantage/-s
"Rowboss hab exwantage mo'nuh fiel'han'."

(A rowboss has more advantages than a fieldhand.)

exwice
(EX-wice) *n.* advice
"Uh g'em exwice 'cep'm dem ent pay no min'."
(I gave them advice but they did not pay attention to me.)

'e yeye duh leak
(e YEYE duk LEAK) *id.* he/she/it is crying
"'E bex 'tell 'e yeye duh leak."
(She is so mad she is crying.)

ez
(EZ) *conj.* as
"De well dry ez uh bone."
(The well is as dry as a bone.)

F

faa'm
(FAAM) *n.* farm/-s
"Uh wu'k tuh Mistuh Towle faa'm."
(I work on Mister Towle's farm.)

faa'myaa'd
(FAAM-yaad) *n.* farmyard/-s
"'Nuf animal tuh de faa'myaa'd."
(There are many animals in the farmyard.)

fack trute
(fack TRUTE) *n.* actual fact; absolute truth
"Uh yent t'ief de hog; dat de fack trute."
(I did not steal the hog; that's the truth.)

'f'aid
(FAID) *adj.* afraid
"Joe 'f'aid de dog."
(Joe is afraid of the dog.)

fait'
(FAIT) *n.* faith
"'E done los' 'e fait' een um."
(She has lost her faith in them.)

fait'ful
(FAIT-ful) *adj.* faithful
"Oonuh kin trus'um fuh fait'ful."
(You can trust them to be faithful.)

fambly
(FAM-bly) *n.* family, families
"Dem hab uh berry laa'ge fambly."
(They have a very large family.)

farruh
(FAR-RUH) *n.* father/-s
"Uh gone 'long me farruh."
(I went with my father.)
NOTE: THE WORD PA IS FREQUENTLY USED FOR FATHER.

farruhlaw
(FAR-ruh-LAW) *n.* father-in-law
"Me farruhlaw he'lt' berry po'ly."
(My father-in-law's health is very poor.)

fas'
(FAS) *adv.* fast; rapidly
"Buh Rabbit run fas', same lukkuh deah."
(Brother Rabbit runs fast, like a deer.)

fas'n
(FAS-'N) *v.* fasten/-s/-ed/-ing
"Fas'n de gyaa'd'n gate."
(Fasten the garden gate.)

fas'n 'e yeye 'pun'top'um
(FAS-'N e yeye pun-TOP-um) *id.* stare in curiosity
"De gal peruse 'roun' fuh mek de man fas'n 'e yeye 'pun'top'um."
(The girl walked slowly around to make the man notice her.)

fat
(FAT) *adj.* prosperous
"Miss Sarah done fuh fat."
(Miss Sarah is very wealthy.)

fat'n 'e yeye
(FAT-'n e yeye) *id.* feast the eyes
"'E fat'n 'e yeye 'pun de bittle."
(He enjoyed the sight of the food.)

fau't
(FAUT) *v.* find fault; criticize
"De 'ooman fau't de Pastuh."
(The woman found fault with the Pastor.)

fawk
(FAWK) *n.* fork
"De gyap stan' dey dey tuh de road fawk."
(The opening in the fence is right there in the fork of the road.)

fawty
(FAW-ty) *adj.* forty
"De mule cos' fawty dolluh."
(The mule cost forty dollars.)

feebuh
(FEE-buh) *n.* fever
"De chile hab chill en' feebuh."
(The child has chills and fever.)

Febbywerry
(FEB-BY-WER-RY) *PN.* February
"'E lef' de two week een Febbywerry munt' done gone."
(She left the second week this past February.)

fedduh
(FED-duh) *n.* feather/-s
"Oonuh mus' sabe de chicken fedduh fuh mek pilluh."
(You must save the chicken feathers to make pillows.")

feed-up
(FEED-up) *v.* feed the horses, mules, cows, etc.
"Bill feed-up 'fo' 'e gone."
(Bill fed the animals before he left.)

'fen'
(FEN) *v.* defend/-s/-ed/-ing
"Ma shoot de dog fuh 'fen'

'ese'f."
(Mother shot the dog to defend herself.)

fench
(FENCH) *n.* fence/-s
"Tek boa'd en' men' de fench."
(Take boards and mend the fence.)

fetch-home
(FETCH-home) *id.* go home; come home
"Sistuh wan' fetch-home."
(Sister wants to come home.)

fiah
(FIAH) *n.* fire/-s
"Bil' uh fiah 'neet' de washpot."
(Build a fire under the washpot.)

fibe
(FIBE) *adj.* five
"De mule een 'e fibe yeah."
(The mule is five years old.)

fiddluh
(FIDD-luh) *n.* fiddler/-s
"De fiddluh play fuh de chillun dance."
(The fiddler played for the children to dance.)

fiel'
(FIEL) *n.* field/-s
"'E gone fiel' fuh folluh mule."
(He went to the field to plow.)

fiel'han'
(FIEL-han) *n.* field hand/-s
"Fiel'han' haffuh wu'k 'tell de sun gone down."
(Field hands have to work until the sun goes down.)

fin'
(FIN) *v.* find/-s, found, finding; give/gave birth
"Ma fin' de hen nes'."
(Mother found the hen's nest.)
"De cow fin' uh cyaaf."
(The cow gave birth.)

fin'lly at las'
(FIN-lly at LAS) *adv.* at last
"Fin'lly at las' uh done'um."
(At last I have finished it.)

fin'um een bittle
(FIN-em een BIT-TLE) *id.* supply food for them
"Pa agguhnize 'e bone fuh fin'um een bittle."
(Father worked until he was bone tired to get food for them.)

fin'um so
(FIN-em so) *id.* found him/her/it in that condition
"Uh yent bruk de hoe; Uh fin'um so."
(I didn't break the hoe; I found it broken.)

fis'
(FIS) *n.* fist/-s
"'E box'um wid 'e fis'."
(He hit him with his fist.)

flabuh
(FLA-buh) *n.* flavor, flavoring
"Pit some buhniluh flabuh een

de cake."
(Put some vanilla flavoring in the cake.)

flam
(FLAM) *v.* hit; kick
"De mule flam de boy good-fashi'n."
(The mule kicked the boy hard.)

flame
(FLAME) *n.* phlegm
"'E hab uh flame een 'e t'roat."
(He has phlegm in his throat.)

flash
(FLASH) *v.* splash/-es/-ed/-ing
"De watuh flash een me face."
(The water splashed in my face.)

flash-'bout
(flash-BOUT) *v.* socialize; have fun
"Dat gal ent study wu'k; 'e too lub fuh flash-'bout."
(That girl doesn't think about work; she likes to have fun.)

flatfawm
(FLAT-fawm) *n.* platform/-s
"Uh bil' de flatfawm tuh de chu'ch."
(I built the platform at the church.)

fling tuh de side
(FLING tuh de SIDE) *id.* gathered on one side—said of a dress or skirt
"Uh wan' de sku't long en' fling tuh de side."
(I want the skirt long and gathered on one side.)

fludduh-fedduh
(FLUD-duh-FED-duh) *id.* rush around aimlessly, like the proverbial chicken with its head cut off
"Dat 'ooman alltime duh fludduh-fedduh."
(That woman is always fluttering around.)

flo'
(FLO) *n.* floor/-s
"Mek'ace en' bresh up de flo'."
(Hurry and sweep the floor.)

flo'clawt'
(FLO-clawt) *n.* a cloth for scrubbing the floor; a mop
"De flo'clawt' dey dey een de cawnuh."
(The mop is there in the corner.)

fly'way
(FLY-way) *n.* a type of hat stylish during the 1930s
"Dem buy fly'way en' shoesh."
(They bought flyaway hats and shoes.)

fo'
(FO) *adj.* four
"Uh mek fo' dolluh."
(I made four dollars.)

'fo'
(FO) *adv.* before
"Uh bin dey 'fo' daa'k."

(I was there before dark.)

'fo' gun-shoot
(FO-gun-shoot) *id.* before the Civil War
"Slab'ry bin yuh 'fo' gun-shoot."
(There was slavery before the Civil War.)

fol'
(FOL) *v.* fold/-s/-ed/-ing
"Dem bin fol' clothes w'en Uh git yuh."
(They were folding clothes when I got here.)

folluh-mule
(fol-luh-MULE) *v.* [follow mule]; plow [with a mule]
"'E bin folluh-mule sence dayclean."
(He has been plowing since daylight.)

fool-up-wid
(fool-UP-wid) *id.* flirt with
"Uh done tell oonuh mus' don' fool-up-wid dat gal."
(I have already told you not to flirt with that girl.)

fo'punce
(FO-punce) *adj.* four pence
"Nyam de fo'punce chickin; lef' de seb'n'punce chickin fuh lay laa'ge aig."
(Eat the four pence chicken; leave the seven pence chicken to lay large eggs.)

foot hasty
(FOOT hast-y) *adj.* anxious to begin
"Oonuh foot hasty, enty?"
(You are anxious to get started, aren't you?)

foot tie tuh de groun'
(FOOT tie tuh de GROUN) *id.* unable to move
"De man so 'f'aid 'e foot tie tuh de groun'."
(The man is so afraid he can't move.)

fo'teen
(FO-teen) *adj.* fourteen
"Ma hab fo'teen chillun."
(Mother had fourteen children.)

freehan'
(FREE-han) *adj.* freehanded; generous
"'E freehan' 'long 'e exwice."
(He is generous with his advice.)

freehan' 'long 'e mout'
(FREE-han long e mout) *id.* very talkative
"Dat gal berry freehan' 'long 'e mout'."
(That girl is very talkative.)

freemale
(FREE-male) *adj.* female
"Me freemale niece bin tuh chu'ch."
(My female niece was at church.)

frizzle-chickin
(FRIZ-ZLE-chick-in) *n.* a chicken on which the feathers stand upright, as if

it backed out of its shell
"Uh gwi' sabe dat frizzle-
chickin fuh show'out."
(I'm going to save that frizzled
chicken to show off.)

fros'
(FROS) *n.* frost
"De hebby fros' kill de tettuh."
(The heavy frost killed the
potatoes.)

fry-bakin
(FRY-bak-in) *n.* fried bacon;
pork meat, from the side of
the hog, cut thin and fried
"Fry-bakin stan' berry good
fuh nyam 'long aig en'
hom'ny."
(Fried bacon is very good to
eat with eggs and hominy.)

fudduh
(FUD-duh) *adv.* further;
farther
"Me gyap stan' fudduh f'um
de big road."
(The road to my house is
farther from the highway.)

fuh
(FUH) *prep.* for; to
"'E gwine home fuh cook
suppuh."
(She is going home to cook
supper.)

fuhgit
(FUH-git) *v.* forget/-s, forgot,
forgetting
"Uh fuhgit weh Uh lef' me
shoesh."
(I forgot where I left my shoes.)

fuh hab
(fuh HAB) *id.* to hold
"Uh picnic bin fuh hab Sat'd'y
done gone, 'cep'm 'e
wedduh."
(A picnic was to have been
held last Saturday, but it
rained.)

fuhrebbuh
(fuhr-EB-BUH) *adv.* forever;
always
"Buh Joe fuhrebbuh duh fish
de crick."
(Brother Joe is always fishing
in the creek.)

fuhr'um
(FUHR-um) *id.* for him/her/it/
them
"Uh gone fuhr'um 'cep'm dey
ent wan' come."
(I went for them but they
didn't want to come.)

fuh sho'
(fuh SHO) *adv.* for sure;
surely
"Uh figguh dem gwi' come
fuh sho'."
(I figured they would surely
come.)

fuh sutt'n
(fuh SUTT-'N) *adv.* for
certain; certainly
"Dem gwi' come tuhreckly,
fuh sutt'n."
(Certainly they will come
directly.)

fuh true
(fuh TRUE) *adv.* [for true];

Virginia Mixson Geraty 45

truly; truthfully
"Uh yent shum, fuh true."
(I haven't seen them, truly.)

fuh who las' de longis'
(fuh who LAS de LONG-is) *id.* until the better man wins
"Dem gwi' fight fuh who las' de longis'."
(They will fight until the better man wins.)

ful'hus
(FUL-hus) *n.* a covered roosting place for fowl
"De fowl roos' een de ful'hus."
(The fowl roost in the fowl house.)

full
(FULL) *v.* fill/-s/-ed/-ing
"Ma duh full de cup wid milk."
(Mother is filling the cup with milk.)

full'up
(FULL-up) *v.* overcome
"De man full'up wid bex."
(The man was overcome with anger.)

f'um
(FUM) *prep.* from
"Git 'way f'um yuh!"
(Get away from here!)

f'um dayclean tuh fus' daa'k
(fum DAY-CLEAN tuh FUS daak) *id.* from sunup to sundown; the entire day
"Uh wu'k f'um dayclean tuh fus' daa'k."
(I have worked from daylight to dusk.)

f'um Rebus tuh Rebulashun
(fum RE-BUS tuh reb-u-LA-SHUN) *id.* from Genesis to Revelation; from beginning to end
"Uh study 'bout'um f'um Rebus tuh Rebulashun."
(I have thought about it from beginning to end.)

fus'
(FUS) *adv.* first
"Dat hen lay fus'."
(That hen was the first to lay.)

fus' daa'k
(FUS daak) *n.* first dark; dusk; sundown; twilight
"Us knock off fus' daa'k."
(We stopped working at dusk.)
NOTE: SEE ALSO *CANDL' LIGHT'N', DUS',* AND *SUN-LEAN FUH DOWN.*

fus' fowl crow
(FUS fowl crow) *n.* the time before daylight when roosters crow
"De dance las' 'tell fus' fowl crow."
(The dance lasted until just before daylight.)

fus' gwinin' off
(fus gwin-in OFF) *id.* in the beginning
"Fus' gwinin' off, de Lawd mek Mistuh Adam."
(In the beginning, the Lord made Mister Adam.)

fus' news 'e know
    (FUS news e KNOW) *id.* the next thing he knew
    "De mule kick Buh Joe en' de fus' news 'e know 'e bin een de hawspittle."
    (The mule kicked Brother Joe and the next thing he knew he was in the hospital.)

G

gabble
    (GAB-ble) *v.* talk rapidly
    "Dem gal gabble same lukkuh goose."
    (Those girls gabble just like geese.)

'gage
    (GAGE) *v.* engaged; pledged
    "Bell 'gage fuh marri'd Rufus."
    (Bell is engaged to marry Rufus.)

gal-chile
    (GAL-chile) *n.* girl child
    "De gal-chile bawn Sat'd'y."
    (The baby girl was born Saturday.)

gal-chillun
    (GAL-chil-lun) *n.* girl children; girls; daughters
    "Uh hab six head ub gal-chillun."
    (I have six girls.)

Gawd-ack
    (GAWD-ACK) *PN.* act of God; natural catastrophe
    "Gawd-ack tek de house."
    (The hurricane destroyed the house.)

Gawd-acre
    (GAWD-acre) *n.* a cemetery
    "'E duh sleep tuh Gawd-acre."
    (She is sleeping in the cemetery.)

Gawd full me jaw teet' wid lie fuh fool de Buckruh.
    id. God has given me the ability to fool the white people.

Gawd mek'um fuh
    (GAWD mek-um fuh) *id.* God made him/her/it for
    "Gawd mek'um fuh tell lie."
    (God created him to tell lies.)

Gawd mek'um, Gawd tek'um, t'engk Gawd.
    (Gawd MEK-UM Gawd TEK-UM tengk GAWD) *id.* God made him; God took him; thank God.

Gawd t'row Him shadduh obuh de Eart'
    (GAWD trow him SHAD-DUH obuh de EART) *id.* God has thrown His shadow over the Earth. The sun has gone down.

gedduh
    (GED-duh) *v.* gather/-s/-ed/-ing
    "'Nuf gal gedduh tuh de sto'."
    (Many girls gathered at the store.)

gedduh tuhgedduh
(GED-DUH tuh-GED-DUH) *v.*
gather very closely together
"De chickin gedduh tuhgedduh 'neet' de house."
(The chickens gathered closely together under the house.)

g'em
(GEM) *v.* give/-s, gave, giving him/her/it/them
"Pa g'em de hog."
(Father gave them the hog.)

'gen
(GEN) *adv.* again
"'E gone fuh shum 'gen."
(He went to see them again.)

'gens'
(GENS) *prep.* against
"De hoe dey dey 'gens' de fench."
(The hoe is right there against the fence.)

gib
(GIB) *v.* give/-s, gave, giving
"Uh gib de Pastuh fibe dolluh."
(I gave the Pastor five dollars.)

gimme
(GIM-me) *v.* give/-s, gave, giving me
"Gimme ten cent wu't' ub candy."
(Give me ten cents worth of candy.)

girt'
(GIRT) *n.* girth
"De girt' bruk."
(The girth is broken.)

git 'e de't'
(GIT e DET) *v.* die/-s/-d, dying
"'E git 'e de't' w'en de hawss t'row'um."
(He died when the horse threw him.)

git een milk
(git een MILK) *id.* ripen/-s
"De cawn done git een milk."
(The corn is ripe.)

git 'e han' een
(GIT e HAN een) *id.* get his/her hands in; become accustomed to; get the hands used to
"Gally min' de baby fuh git 'e han' een."
(Gally took care of the baby so she could become accustomed to the work.)

git hitch
(git HITCH) *v.* marry, married
"Joe en' Mina git hitch de two Sat'd'y done gone."
(Joe and Mina married two weeks ago this Saturday.)

git 'ligun
(git LI-GION) *v.* get religion; be baptized
"Dat seek'n' sistuh git 'ligun."
(That sister wanting religion was baptized.)

git't'ru
(git-TRU) *v.* get through; finish; complete

"'E git't'ru men' de fench en' gone."
(He finished mending the fence and left.)

git 'way
(git WAY) *interj.* get away
"Git 'way f'um yuh!"
(Get away from here!)

gi'we
(GI-we) *v.* give/-s, gave, giving to us
"Dem gi'we some bittle."
(They gave us some food.)

'gleck
(GLEC) *v.* neglect
"De pastuh suh mus' don' 'gleck de grabe."
(The pastor said not to neglect the grave.)

glub
(GLUB) *n.* glove/-s
"Pa los' one 'e glub."
(Father lost one of his gloves.)

gone-'cross
(gone-CROSS) *v.* [gone across]; died
"Bubbuh gone-'cross een Augus' munt'."
(Brother died in August.)

gone een
(gone EEN) *id.* go home or to the hospital to have a baby
"Sistuh gone een yistiddy."
(Sister went home yesterday to have her baby.)

gone-grabe
(gone-GRAVE) *v.* visit the grave/cemetery
"Ma, dem, gone-grabe."
(Mother and the others have gone to the cemetery to visit the graves.)

gone-hookhan'
(gone-HOOK-han) *v.* walk arm in arm
"Della en' Joe gone-hookhan' 'long de paat'."
(Della and Joe walked arm in arm along the path.)

gone tuh 'ese'f
(GONE tuh E-SEF) *id.* leave present company in order to attend to personal matters
"De gal lef' de fiel' fuh gone tuh 'ese'f."
(The girl left the field to attend to personal matters.)

gonnil
(GON-nil) *n.* gunwale
"De wabe come obuh de boat gonnil."
(The waves came over the boat's gunwale.)

good-fashi'n
(GOOD-fash-i'n) *adv.* throughly
"'E resplain good-fashi'n how fuh do'um."
(He explained exactly how to do it.)

gots
(GOTS) *v.* is compelled; must

"'E suh 'e ma call'um; 'e gots tuh go."
(He said his mother called him; he has to go.)

gouch
(GOUCH) *n.* gout
"'E duh leddown 'kase 'e hab gouch."
(She is lying down because she has gout.)

grabble
(GRAB-ble) *n.* gravel
"T'row de grabble 'cross de paat'."
(Put the gravel on the path.)

grabble
(GRAB-ble) *v.* dig/-s, dug, digging
"Uh grabble tettuh f'um dayclean 'tell daa'k."
(I dug potatoes from daylight to dark.)

grabe
(GRABE) *n.* grave/-s
"Dey pit 'e cheer 'pun'top 'e grabe."
(They put his chair on top of his grave.)
NOTE: THE CHAIR AND OTHER FAVORITE BELONGINGS WERE PLACED ON THE GRAVE OF THE DECEASED SO THAT HE/SHE WOULD HAVE NO OCCASION TO COME BACK TO THE HOUSE.

grabeyaa'd
(GRABE-yaad) *n.* graveyard/-s
"De grabeyaa'd dey dey tuh de chu'ch."
(The graveyard is right there at the church.)

graff
(GRAFF) *v.* grab/-s/-ed/-ing
"De boy duh graff de gal aa'm."
(The boy is grabbing the girl's arm.)

granny
(GRAN-ny) *n.* an old woman; a midwife
"De granny bring de baby 'fo' de doctuh git yuh."
(The midwife delivered the baby before the doctor came.)

grano
(GRAN-o) *n.* guana; manufactured fertilizer
"Pit 'nuf grano 'long de cawn."
(Put plenty of fertilizer on the corn.)

'gree
(GREE) *v.* agree/-s/-ed/-ing
"Dem two gal ent nebbuh 'gree."
(Those two girls have never agreed.)

greebe
(GREEBE) *v.* grieve/-s/-ed/-ing
"Pa done dead dese ten yeah, stillyet Ma duh greebe fuhr'um."
(Father has been dead for ten years, still Mother is grieving for him.)

gree'bunce hab'um
  (GREE-bunce HAB-um) *id.*
  grief has him/her/them; they
  are overcome with grief
  "Gree'bunce hab'um, fuh true."
  (They are truly overcome with
  grief.)

'greement
  (gree-MENT) *n.* agreement/-s
  "Uh mek 'greement fuh buy de
  lan'."
  (I made an agreement to buy
  the land.)

greese 'e mout'
  (greese e MOUT) *id.* improve
  the taste
  "Stir 'nuf buttuh een de
  hom'ny fuh greese 'e mout'."
  (Stir enough butter into the
  hominy to improve the
  taste.)

grin'salt
  (GRIN-salt) *id.* the circling of
  a scavenger over its prey
  "'E duh grin'salt fuh nyam
  'long'um."
  (He is grinding salt to eat with
  it.)

gritch
  (GRITCH) *n.* grits
  "Bile de gritch fuh we
  suppuh."
  (Boil the grits for our supper.)

groan een 'e sperrit
  GROAN een e SPER-RIT) *id.*
  groan in the spirit; mourn
  "'E yent mek hebby complain,
  stillyet 'e groan een 'e
  sperrit."
  (She didn't voice her grief,
  still she mourned.)

groun'
  (GROUN) *n.* ground
  "New groun' ent mek good
  crap."
  (Ground that hasn't been
  planted before does not
  produce good crops.)

gubmunt
  (GUB-munt) *n.* government
  "De gubmunt done tek all us
  money fuh tax."
  (The government has taken all
  our money for taxes.)

gumball
  (GUM-ball) n. gumboil/-s
  "Joe gone doctuh fuh see 'bout
  'e gumball."
  (Joe went to the doctor to see
  about his gumboil.)

gum-up
  (GUM-up) *v.* gummed up;
  smeared
  "De chile face gum-up wid
  swee'tettuh."
  (The child's face is smeared
  with sweet potato.)

gunjuh
  (GUN-juh) *n.* cake made with
  molasses
  "Ma cook gunjuh for suppuh."
  (Mother cooked a cake made
  with molasses for supper.)

gwi'
  (GWI) *v.* is/are going

"'E gwi' shoot bu'd."
(He is going to shoot birds.)

gwine
(GWINE) *v.* is/are going
"De gal gwine chu'ch."
(The girls are going to church.)
NOTE: *GWI'* AND *GWINE* ARE INTERCHANGEABLE. *GWI'* IS GENERALLY USED WHEN THE SPEAKER IS IN A HURRY.

gyaa'd
(GYAAD) *v.* guard/-s/-ed/-ing
"Dey lef' de dog fuh gyaa'd de house."
(They left the dog to guard the house.)

gyaa'd'n
(GYAAD-'n) *n.* garden/-s
"Maum Chrish' duh wu'k 'e gyaa'd'n."
(Maum Chrish is working in her garden.)

gyap
(GYAP) *n.* any gap or opening in a fence, such as a gate; a road or path leading from the highway to a private home
"Uh lef'um tuh 'e gyap."
(I left him at the path leading to his house.)

gyap
(GYAP) *v.* yawn/-s/-ed/-ing
"De chile duh gyap; 'e sleepy tuh dat."
(The child is yawning; he is that sleepy.)

H

haa'bis'
(HAA-bis) *n.* harvest/-s
"De haa'bis' done gedduh."
(The harvest is already gathered.)

haa'bis'
(HAA-bis) *v.* harvest/-s/-ed/-ing
"Dey haa'bis' de crap een Octobuh munt'."
(They harvested the crop in October.)

haa'buh
(HAA-buh) *n.* harbor/-s
"De mens, dem, gone tuh de haa'buh fuh fish."
(The men and the others went to the harbor to fish.)

haa'd
(HAAD) *adj.* hard
"De tree too haa'd fuh chop."
(The tree is too hard to chop.)

haa'd-bile
(HAAD-bile) *adj.* hard-boiled
"Chop up uh haa'd-bile aig en' pit'um een de graby."
(Chop a hard-boiled egg and put it in the gravy.)

haa'd-head
(HAAD-head) adj. hardheaded
"Miss Ebe bin berry haa'd-head."
(Miss Eve was very hardheaded.)

haa'dly'kin
(HAAD-ly-kin) *id.* [hardly can]; is barely able
"'E haa'dly'kin moobe 'bout."
(She is barely able to move about.)

haa'kee
(HAAK-ee) *v.* hark; listen
"Uh yeddy 'cep'm Uh yent haa'kee."
(I heard but I didn't listen.)

haa'ness
(HAA-ness) *n.* harness/-es
"De mule haa'ness racktify."
(The mule's harness is broken.)

haa'ness
(HAA-ness) *v.* harness/-es/-ed/-ing
"Joe haa'ness de mule tuh de plow."
(Joe harnessed the mule to the plow.)

haant
(HAANT) *n.* ghost/-s
"De haant bin walk de paa't."
(The ghost was walking the path.)

haant
(HAANT) *v.* torment
"Hag haant we eb'ry night."
(Hags haunt us every night.)

haa't
(HAAT) *n.* heart/-s
"Me haa't hebby."
(My heart is heavy. I am very depressed.)

haa't'
(HAAT) *n.* hearth/-s
"Tek out de ashish en' bresh de haa't'."
(Take out the ashes and brush off the hearth.)

haa't stan'
(HAAT stan) *id.* attitude is; belief is
"Me haa't stan' same lukkuh de buckruh."
(My belief is the same as the white people.)

haa'ty wilcum
(HAAT-Y wil-come) *interj.* hearty welcome; a salutation
"Haa'ty wilcum tuh oonuh."
(A hearty welcome to you.)

hab
(HAB) *v.* has, have, had, having
"'E hab febuh."
(She has a fever.)

hab chile
(hab CHILE) *v.* gave birth
"'E hab chile 'fo' fus' daa'k."
(She had the baby before sundown.)

hab mis'ry
(hab MIS-ry) *id.* has/have misery; has/have pain
"Pa hab mis'ry een 'e j'int."
(Father has pain in his joints.)

hab sin
(hab SIN) *id.* has/have sin; is/are guilty
"Dem wuh t'ief hab sin."

(Those who steal are guilty.)

hab strong pocket
(hab STRONG pock-et) *id.*
has/have a strong pocket; is/are wealthy
"Man ent t'row 'way 'ooman wuh hab strong pocket."
(A man doesn't divorce a woman who is wealthy.)

hab uh nyung nachuh
(hab uh NYUNG na-chuh) *id.*
has/have a young nature; possessing the attitude of a young person
"Bubbuh hab uh nyung nachuh."
(Brother acts like a young man.)

haffuh
(HAF-fuh) *v.* has/have to
"Uh haffuh wu'k berry haa'd."
(I have to work very hard.)

haffuh 'cratch 'roun'
(haf-fuh CRATCH roun) *id.*
has/have to scratch around; has/have to struggle
"Joe haffuh 'cratch 'roun' fuh mek uh libb'n."
(Joe has to struggle to make a living.)

haffuh hasty
(haf-fuh HAS-TY) *id.* has/have to make haste; has/have to hurry
"Uh haffuh hasty fuh ketch dat strain."
(I have to hurry to catch that train.)

haffuh schemy
(haf-fuh SCHEM-Y) *id.* has/have to come up with a scheme
"Uh haffuh schemy fuh ketch dat chickin t'ief."
(I have to come up with a scheme to catch that chicken thief.)

hag-holluh
(HAG hol-luh) *n.* after midnight; that time of night when you can hear hags calling
"Uh git home 'fo' hag-holluh."
(I got home before midnight.)

half-han'
(HALF-han) *n.* half-hand; a child worker
"Uh half-han' mek half wage."
(A child worker makes half the salary of an adult.)

hambone
(HAM-bone) *n.* rhythmic movements and sounds made by a person slapping his/her hands against parts of the body, primarily the thighs
"De chile mo' bettuh tuh de hambone dan 'e Ma."
(The child is better at hambone than her mother.)

hampuh
(HAMP-uh) *v.* hamper; hinder
"De boy cyan' walk; 'e bruk toe hampuhr'um."
(The boy can't walk; his broken toe hampers him.)

han'
(HAN) *n.* hand/-s; worker/-s
"'E han' du'tty."
(His hands are dirty.)
"De han' done bin pay off."
(The workers have already received their wages.)

han'
(HAN) *v.* hand/-s/-ed/-ing; give/-s, gave, giving
"Han' de pot yuh."
(Give the pot [here] to me.)

hanch
(HANCH) *n.* haunch/-es; hind quarter of an animal
"De dog bite de cow hanch."
(The dog bit the cow's haunch.)

han'hasty
(han-HAST-Y) *adv.* [hand hasty]; quick
"'E han'hasty fuh t'ief."
(He is quick to steal.)

hankuh
(HAN-kuh) *v.* hanker; crave; desire
"Miss Ebe hankuh attuh dat apple."
(Miss Eve craved that apple.)

han' short pashunt
(han short PA-SHUNT) *id.* hand is short of patience, quick to strike
"Ma knock de chile; 'e han' short pashunt."
(Mother hit the child; she is short of patience.)

han' t'read
(han TREAD) *n.* hand thread; thread used for sewing by hand
"Della gone sto' fuh buy han' t'read."
(Della went to the store to buy [hand] thread.)

happ'n 'long
(HAPP-'N long) *v.* drop in; visit unexpectedly
"Dem happ'n 'long fuh wissit."
(They visited unexpectedly.)

harricane
(HARR-Y-CANE) *n.* hurricane/-s
"De harricane blow de shed down."
(The hurricane blew down the shed.)

harricane tree
(HARR-Y-cane TREE) *n.* a tree that has been uprooted by a storm
"De harricane tree fall 'pun'top de fench."
(The tree, uprooted by the storm, fell on the fence.)

harruh
(HAR-ruh) *n.* harrow/-s
"Alltwo de harruh dey tuh de baa'n."
(Both the harrows are there in the barn.)

harruh
(HAR-ruh) *v.* harrow/-s/-ed/-ing
"Pa duh harruh de lan'."

Virginia Mixson Geraty

(Father is harrowing the land.)

harrydick
(HAR-RY-dick) *n.* young bull/-s
"Mus' don' nebbuh fench-up de harrydick."
(You must never fence the young bulls together.)

hasslet
(HASS-let) *n.* the edible internal organs of a butchered animal
"Bile de hasslet fuh mek graby."
(Boil the hasslets to make gravy.)
NOTE: ALTHOUGH THIS IS AN ENGLISH WORD, I HAD NEVER HEARD IT UNTIL MY GULLAH INFORMANT USED IT.

hasty
(HAS-TY) *adj.* anxious
"Oonuh hasty fuh gone, enty?"
(You are anxious to go, aren't you?")

hatchitch
(HATCH-itch) *n.* hatchet/-s
"De hatchitch cos' two dolluh."
(The hatchet costs two dollars.)

hawn
(HAWN) *n.* horn/-s
"Alltwo de goat hawn bruk off."
(Both the goat's horns are broken off.)

hawn'owl
(HAWN-owl) *n.* horned owl/-s

"De hawn'owl duh 'pread 'e wing."
(The horned owl is spreading his wings.)

hawss
(HAWSS) *n.* horse/-s
"Hitch up de hawss tuh de cyaa't."
(Hitch the horse up to the cart.)

head'n'
(HEAD-'n) *n.* heading/-s; small drainage ditch
"W'en de rain hol'up, Joe gwi' cut head'n' een de fiel'."
(When the rain stops, Joe will cut drainage ditches in the field.)

head-off
(HEAD-off) *v.* leave to go to a particular place
"Dem head-off fuh towng."
(They left to go to town.)

head tek 'way
(HEAD tek WAY) *id.* lose/lost one's mind
"Dat 'ooman head tek 'way."
(That woman has lost her mind.)

heap'uh howdy
(HEAP-uh howd-y) *n.* heap of howdy; a hearty welcome
"Uh g'em heap'uh howdy."
(I gave them a hearty welcome.)

heap'uh time
(HEAP-UH time) *id.* heap of

times; many times
"Heap'uh time uh gone duh ribbuh tuh fish."
(Many times I have gone to the river to fish.)

hebby
(HEB-by) *adj.* heavy; to a great extent
"'E haa't hebby, 'e lonesome tuh dat."
(She is so lonesome, she has a heavy heart.)

hebby belly
(HEB-BY BEL-LY) *n.* [heavy belly]; a great appetite
"Bubbuh hab hebby belly fuh fish."
(Bubbuh has a great appetite for fish [or fishing].)

hebby dry drought
(heb-by DRY drought) *id.* a long period of dry weather
"De hebby dry drought 'mos' racktify de cawn."
(The long drought almost ruined the corn.)

hebby he'lt'
(heb-by HELT) *n.* good health
"Dem eenj hebby he'lt'."
(They are enjoying good health.)

hebby wet drought
(heb-by WET drought) *id.* a long period of wet weather
"De hebby wet drought 'mos' racktify de cawn."
(The continued rain almost ruined the corn.)

heb'nly
(HEB-'N-ly) *adj.* heavenly
"Praise de Heb'nly Farruh!"
(Praise the Heavenly Father!)

he'lt'
(HELT) *n.* health
"Pa eenjy berry po' he'lt'."
(Father enjoys very poor health.)

heng
(HENG) *v.* hang/-s/-ed/-ing, *also* hung
"Dem heng de clothes 'pun'top de fench."
(They hung the clothes on the fence.)

hengkitchuh
(HENG-kitch-uh) *n.* handkerchief/-s
"Chile, tie-up dat money een you hengkitchuh."
(Child, tie that money in your handkerchief.)

hice
(HICE) *v.* hoist; lift
"W'en Uh shum dat snake, Uh hice me frock en' run."
(When I saw that snake, I lifted my dress and ran.)

hice de chune
(HICE de CHUNE) *id.* [hoist the tune]; start the song/singing
"Buh Joe hice de chune."
(Brother Joe started the singing.)

hick'ry'nott
(hick-ry-NOTT) *n.* hickory nut
"De squarril hab uh hick'ry'nott."
(The squirrel has a hickory nut.)

Higguhri-hee
(HIG-guh-ri-HEE) *PN.* horned owl/-s
"Uh tremble, fuh true, w'en uh yeddy de Higguhri-hee."
(Truly, I tremble when I hear the horned owl.)
NOTE: *HIGGUHRI-HEE* IS THE SOUND MADE BY THE GREAT HORNED OWL. THE SOUNDS MADE BY ANIMALS AND BIRDS ARE OFTEN USED BY GULLAH SPEAKERS TO NAME THEM.

high-buckruh
(HIGH-buck-ruh) *n.* upper-class white person/-s; wealthy white person/-s
"De high-buckruh hab big paa'ty tuh dem house."
(The rich white people had a big party at their house.)

him
(HIM) *pron.* he/she/it, his/hers/its
"Dis one fuh him."
(This one is hers.)

him'own
(HIM-own) *pron.* his/her/its own
"De cyaa't him'own."
(The cart is his own.)

hin'
(HINE) *adj.* hind
"De dog bruk 'e hin' foot."
(The dog broke his hind foot.)

hin'quawtuh
(HIN-quaw-tuh) *n.* hindquarter
"De buckruh gib we de gam; demse'f nyam de hin'quawtuh."
(The white people gave us the front quarter, they ate the hindquarter themselves.)

hip'n
(HIP-'N) *n.* diaper/-s
"Fix de chile hip'n!"
(Fix the child's diaper!)

hippycrick
(HIP-PY-crick) n. hypocrite/-s
"Dat hippycrick duh onrabble 'e mout'."
(That hypocrite is rambling at great length.)

historicuss
(his-TOR-I-cuss) *adj.* historical
"'Lizabet' study uh historicuss book duh school."
(Elizabeth studies a history book at school.)

hoe-han'le-man
(HOE-han-'le-MAN) *n.* a wife beater; a man who beats his wife with a hoe handle
"Uh yeddy Mina git hitch tuh uh hoe-han'le-man."
(I heard Mina married a wife beater.)

hoe man
(HOE man) *n.* a man who hoes
"De rowboss tell de hoe man mus' knock off."
(The foreman told the field hand to stop working.)

hol' cumpuhsayshun
(HOL cum-puh-SAY-shun) *id.* hold conversation; converse/-s/-ed, conversing
"'E hol' cumpuhsayshun 'long'um."
(She conversed with him.)

hol' hoe
(hol' HOE) *v.* [hold a] hoe
"De chile too leetle fuh hol' hoe."
(The child is too young to hoe.)

holluh
(HOL-luh) *n.* hollow, as of a tree
"De coon dey dey duh de holluh."
(The raccoon is right there in the hollow of the tree.)

holluh
(HOL-luh) *v.* holler/-s/-ed/-ing; call out
"Holluh tuhr'um een de house."
(Call to them in the house.)

hol'um cheap
(hol-um CHEAP) *id.* [hold him/her/them cheap]; has/have no respect or regard for someone or something
"'Bram chillun hol'um cheap."
(Abraham's children have no respect for him.)

hom'ny
(HOM-ny) *n.* hominy
"Bile de hom'ny 'tell 'e spit back."
(Boil the hominy until it bubbles and bursts from the pot as if spitting.)

hongry
(HONG-ry) *adj.* hungry
"De hongry chile duh cry."
(The hungry child is crying.)

'hoop en' holluh
(HOOP en HOL-LUH) *v.* whoop and holler; cry out loudly
"W'en de man die, 'e fambly 'hoop en' holluh."
(When the man died, his family cried out loudly.)

Hoppin' John
(HOP-PIN john) *PN.* a dish made with rice and peas cooked together
"All ub we nyam Hoppin' John w'en New Yeah Day come 'roun'."
(All of us eat Hoppin' John on New Year's Day.)

hot
(HOT) *v.* heat/-s/-ed/-ing
"Hot de watuh fuh mek tea."
(Heat the water to make tea.)

huccome
(HUC-come) *adv.* how come; why

"Huccome oonuh ent gwine chu'ch?"
(Why are you not going to church?)

huffuh
(HUF-fuh) *id.* how to
"'E tell'um 'zackly huffuh do'um."
(He told them exactly how to do it.)

hummuch
(HUM-much) *id.* how much; how many
"Hummuch chillun lib duh de faa'm?"
(How many children live on the farm?)

hummuchr'um
(hum-MUCH-'r-um) *id.* how much/many of them
"Hummuchr'um gone tuh school?"
(How many of them go to school?)

hund'ud
(HUND-ud) *adj.* one hundred
"Uh hund'ud en' fo' chillun lib duh de faa'm."
(One hundred and four children live on the farm.)

hu't
(HUT) *v.* hurt/-s/-ing
"Me aa'm duh hu't."
(My arm is hurting.)

I

ib'ry
(IB-ry) *n.* ivy
"Mus' don' cut de ib'ry!"
(Don't cut the ivy!)

i'on
(I-on) *n.* iron
"De w'eel mek ub i'on."
(The wheel is made of iron.)

i'on
(I-on) *v.* iron/-s/-ed/-ing
"Uh haffuh i'on de clothes w'en dem done dry."
(I have to iron the clothes when they have dried thoroughly.)

i'on'n'
(I-on-'n) *n.* ironing; clothes that have been ironed
"Ma cya' de i'on'n' tuh Miss Ray house."
(Mother carried the ironed clothes to Mrs. Ray's house.)

J

jabbuh
(JAB-buh) *v.* jabber/-s/-ed/-ing
"Dat 'ooman jabbuh same lukkuh monkry."
(That woman jabbers just like a monkey.)

Jacky-muh-lantu'n
(JACK-Y-muh-lan-tun) *n.* Jack o' Lantern
"De chile skay'd de Jacky-

muh-lantu'n."
(The child is afraid of the jack o' lantern.)

jallous
(JAl-lus) *adj.* jealous
"'E jallous ub de gal, enty?"
(He is jealous of the girl, isn't he?)

jam-up
(JAM-up) *v.* crowd/-s/-ed/-ing
"W'en de rain staa't, eb'rybody jam-up een de chu'ch."
(When the rain started, everybody crowded into the church.)

jaw duh leak
(jaw duh LEAK) *v.* salivate/-s/-d, salivating
"De dog jaw duh leak, 'e hongry tuh dat."
(The dog is so hungry he is salivating.)

jaw teet' full wid lie
(jaw teet FULL wid lie) *id.*
"'E alltime duh lie. 'E jaw teet' full wid lie."
(He is always lying. His jaw teeth are filled with lies.)

'jeck
(JEC) *v.* reject/-s/-ed/-ing
"Joe wife 'jeck'um."
(Joe's wife rejected him.)

jedge
(JEDGE) *n.* judge/-s
"De jedge fine um fibe dolluh."
(The judge fined him five dollars.)

Jedus
(JE-dus) *PN.* Jesus
"Jedus cyo' de bline man."
(Jesus cured the blind man.)

jew
(JEW) *n.* dew
"Hebby jew dey 'pun'top de groun'."
(There is heavy dew on the ground.)

jine
(JINE) *v.* join/-s/-ed/-ing
"Two gal jine de chu'ch."
(Two girls joined the church.)

j'int
(JINT) *n.* joint/-s
"Uh hab de mis'ry een me j'int."
(I have a pain in my joint.)

j'intgrass
(JINT-grass) *n.* joint grass
"Knock de j'intgrass out de cawn."
(Hoe the joint grass out of the corn.)

Jinnywerry
(JIN-NY-wer-ry) *PN.* January
"Sistuh baby bawn een Jinnywerry munt'."
(Sister's baby was born in January.)

jis'
(JIS) *adv.* just
"Uh gone 'long'um jis' fuh de

Virginia Mixson Geraty

ride."
(I went with them just for the ride.)

jisso
(JIS-so) *adv.* just so; for no particular reason
"Den gone towng jisso."
(They have no particular reason for going to town.)

jook
(JOOK) *v.* jab/-s/-ed/-ing
"Gabe jook de frog wid 'e stick."
(Gabe jabbed the frog with his stick.)

jookass
(JOOK-ASS) *n.* jackass/-es
"Jookass en' mule stan' same fashi'n."
(Jackasses and mules look and act alike.)

jue
(JUE) *n.* dues
"Bubbuh ent pay 'e jue."
(Brother hasn't paid his dues.)

jue
(JUE) *v.* due; expected
"De strain jue 'fo' daa'k."
(The train is due before dark.)

ju'k
(JUK) *v.* jerk/-s/-ed/-ing
"De gal ju'k de cow rope fuh mek'um hasty."
(The girl jerked the cow's rope to make her hurry.)

juntlemun
(JUN-tle-man) *n.* gentleman/-men; a woman's legal husband
"Joe Della juntlemun."
(Joe is Della's husband.)

K

'ka'ce
(KACE) *adj.* scarce
"Dey mek demse'f 'ka'ce."
(They made themselves scarce.)

'ka'cely
(KACE-ly) *adv.* scarcely
"Jeems 'ka'cely git't'ru 'e wu'k 'fo' 'e gone."
(James had scarcely finished before he left.)

Kate
(KATE) *PN.* woodpecker/-s
"De Kate done knock hole een de tree."
(The woodpecker has knocked a hole in the tree.)

ketch
(KETCH) *v.* catch/-es, caught, catching
"Us ketch 'nuffuh crab w'en de tide bin low."
(We caught many crabs when the tide was low.)

kibbuh
(KIB-buh) *n.* cover/-s
"Pit de kibbuh 'pun'top de pot."
(Put a cover on the pot.)

kibbuh
(KIB-buh) *v.* cover/-s/-ed/-ing
"Kibbuh de pot fuh de watuh bile."
(Cover the pot so the water will boil.)

killybash
(KIL-LY-bash) *n.* the gourdlike fruit of the calabash tree
"Full de killybash wid watuh."
(Fill the gourd with water.)

kimbo 'e aa'm
(KIM-bo e aam) *id.* to place the hands on the hips in a show of defiance or resignation
"'E kimbo 'e aa'm; 'e bex duh dat!"
(She put her hands on her hips defiantly; she was so vexed.)
NOTE: THIS GESTURE EXPRESSES DEFIANCE IF THE ELBOWS ARE HELD IN A FORWARD POSITION. IF THE ELBOWS ARE LOWERED, THE GESTURE SHOWS RESIGNATION.

kin
(KIN) *v.* can
"De baby kin stan' 'lone."
(The baby can stand alone.)

kin'
(KIN) *adj.* kind
"De man berry kin' tuh 'e animel."
(The man is very kind to his animals.)

kitn'y
(KIT-ny) *n.* kidney/-s
"Fry kitn'y good fuh nyam 'long rice."
(Fried kidneys are good to eat with rice.)

kittle
(KIT-tle) *n.* kettle/-s
"Full de kittle wid watuh fuh mek tea."
(Fill the kettle with water to make tea.)

kitteny
(KITT-en-y) *n.* kitten/-s
"De maamy cat hab fo' kitteny."
(The mother cat has four kittens.)

knock-grass
(knock-GRASS) *v.* hoe/-d/-ing
"Pa tuh de fiel' duh knock-grass."
(Father is in the field hoeing the grass.)

knock off
(knock-OFF) *v.* stop working
"'E done two tas' 'fo' 'e knock off."
(She did two tasks before she knocked off.)

kyag
(KYAG) *n.* keg/-s
"Joe buy two kyag ub nail."
(Joe bought two kegs of nails.)

kyarrysene
(KYAR-RY-sene) *n.* kerosene
"Full de lantu'n wid kyarrysene."
(Fill the lantern with kerosene.)

L

laa'ceny
 (LAA-cen-y) *n.* larceny
 "De law hab'um fuh laa'ceny."
 (He has been arrested for larceny.)

laa'd
 (LAAD) *n.* lard; shortening
 "Ma gone sto' fuh buy uh laa'ge can ub laa'd."
 (Mother went to the store to buy a large can of lard.)

laa'ge
 (LAAGE) *adj.* large
 "Miss Nell laa'ge fuh true."
 (Truly, Miss Nell is large.)

laa'k
 (LAAK) *n.* lark/-s
 "De two leetle laa'k mek dem nes' een de apple tree."
 (The two little larks made their nest in the apple tree.)

laa'n
 (LAAN) *v.* learn/-s/-ed/-ing; teach/-es, taught, teaching
 "Ma laa'n me fuh weabe w'en uh been uh leetle gal."
 (Mother taught me to weave when I was a little girl.)

laig
 (LA-ig) *n.* leg/-s
 "De bu'd laig bruk."
 (The bird's leg is broken.)

laige
 (LAI-ge) *n.* ledge/-s
 "Set de pot tuh de winduh laige."
 (Put the pot on the window ledge.)

lam
 (LAM) *v.* hit
 "Bubbuh lam de mule duh two time."
 (Brother hit the mule twice.)

lam'quawtuh
 (LAM-quaw-tuh) *n.* lamb's-quarters; white goosefoot
 "Lam'quawtuh berry good fuh nyam."
 (Lamb's-quarters is very good to eat.)

lap-chile
 (LAP-chile) *n.* a child too young to sit alone; children that have to be held
 "Uh yent lub fuh min' lap-chile."
 (I don't like to take care of children that are too young to sit alone.)

lavuh
 (LA-vuh) *v.* labor/-s/-ed/-ing
 "Mistuh Noruh lavuh fuh bil' de aa'k."
 (Mister Noah labored to build the ark.)

lawfully-lady
 (LAW-ful-ly-LAD-Y) *n.* a man's legal wife
 "Della Bram lawfully-lady."
 (Della is Bram's wife.)

leabe
(LEABE) *n.* leaf, leaves
"De tree done los' 'e leabe."
(The tree has lost its leaves.)

leabe
(LEABE) *v.* leave/-s, left, leaving
"Dem leabe 'fo' us git dey."
(They left before we got there.)

lean berry hebby
(lean BER-RY heb-by) *v.* make a sharp turn
"W'en oonuh git tuh de chu'ch, lean berry hebby tuh de lef'."
(When you get to the church, make a sharp turn to the left.)

lean fuh
(LEAN fuh) *id.* go directly to a particular place
"W'en 'e ma call'um, 'e lean fuh home."
(When his mother called him, he went directly home.)

lean fuh down
(lean fuh DOWN) *id.* said of the sun as it begins to set
"De sun lean fuh down."
(The sun is beginning to set.)

lebble
(LEB-BLE) *adj.* level
"Dat lan' ent lebble."
(That land isn't level.)

'leb'n
(LEB-'n) *adj.* eleven
"'Leb'n chillun come fuh play ball."
(Eleven children came to play ball.)

leddown
(LED-down) *v.* lay/lie/lying down
"Pa duh leddown 'neet' de tree."
(Father is lying underneath the tree.)

ledduh
(LED-duh) *n.* leather
"De haa'ness mek ub ledduh."
(The harness is made of leather.)

leek
(LEEK) *v.* lick/-s/-ed/-ing
"De dog leek 'e foot."
(The dog is licking his foot.)

leetle
(LEET-le) *adj.* little
"De leetle gal duh cry."
(The little girl is crying.)

leetle tetch
(LEET-le tetch) *n.* a little touch; a small amount
"Gib' de chile uh leetle tetch ub molasses."
(Give the child a little bit of molasses.)

lef'
(LEF) *v.* leave/-s, left, leaving
"Lef' dat gal 'lone!"
(Leave that girl alone!)

lef'han'
(LEF-han) *adj.* left [hand or

foot]; belonging to the left side of the body
"De man bruk 'e lef'han' foot."
(The man broke his left foot.)

lef'han' buck
(lef-han BUCK) *n.* a left [upper or lower] incisor
"'E lef'han' buck hu't'um."
(He has a pain in his left incisor.)

leh
(LEH) *v.* let
"Pa yent leh Joe gone 'long'um."
(Father did not let Joe go with him.)

leh we
(LEH we) *id.* let us
"Let we go!"
(Let's go!)

le'm
(LEM) *id.* let them
"Dey ax Ma fuh le'm gone."
(They asked Mother to let them go.)

le'm'lone
(lem-LONE) *v.* let him/her/it/them alone
"Ef dem ent wan' gone, le'm'lone."
(If they don't want to go, let them alone.)

len'
(LEN) *v.* lend/-s, lent, lending
"Ma ax'um fuh len'um 'e ax."
(Mother asked im to lend her his ax.)

'less
(LESS) *conj.* unless
"Uh yent gwine 'less dey ax me."
(I'm not going unless they ask me.)

lib
(LIB) *v.* live/-s/-ed/-ing
"Weh 'e liv?"
(Where does he live?)

libbin'
(LIB-bin) *n.* living
"Pa wu'k haa'd fuh mek uh libbin'."
(Father works hard to make a living.)

libbuh
(LIB-BUH) *n.* liver/-s
"Bile de hog libbuh fuh mek cheese."
(Boil the hog liver to make hog head cheese.)

'libbuh
(LIB-BUH) *v.* deliver/-s/-ed/-ing
"Jim done 'libbuh de kin'lin' tuh de sto'."
(Jim has already delivered the wood kindling to the store.)

'libe
(LIBE) *adj.* alive
"De crab bin 'libe w'en uh pit'um een de pot."
(The crabs were alive when I put them in the pot.)

lick
(LICK) *n.* a blow/-s

"Buh Rabbit gib' Buh
Taa'baby uh lick wid 'e
behime foot."
(Brother Rabbit kicked Brother
Tarbaby with his hind foot.

lick back
(LICK BACK) *id.* turn around
quickly and go back
"W'en Bubbuh meet de bull,
'e lick back en' gone home."
(When Brother met the bull, he
turned quickly and went
back home.)

lick up
(LICK UP) *v.* beat, as eggs
"Lick up two aig fuh pit een
de cake."
(Beat two eggs to put in the
cake.)

light on
(LIGHT ON) *v.* reprimand/-s/
-ed/-ing
"Ma light on Sistuh fuh 'e
yent done de wash."
(Mother reprimanded Sister
because she hadn't washed
the clothes.)

light'ood
(LIGHT-ood) *n.* lightwood;
kindling
"Fetch de light'ood fuh staa't
de fiah."
(Bring the lightwood to start
the fire.)

light out
(LIGHT OUT) *id.* leave
hurriedly
"Fus' daa'k 'e light out fuh
home."
(At sundown he left hurriedly
to go home.)

light out attuhr'um
(LIGHT out AT-TUHR-um) *id.*
chase/-s/-d, chasing him/her/
them
"W'en de dog t'ief de chickin,
Ma light out attuhr'um."
(When the dog stole the
chicken, Mother chased
him.)

light sin
(LIGHT sin) *n.* venial sin
"Uh chile wuh tek uh cookie
hab light sin."
(A child who takes a cookie is
guilty of venial sin.)

likeso
(LIKE-so) *adv.* also
"De boy, likeso de gal, t'ief de
apple."
(The boy, and also the girl,
stole the apples.)

linniment
(lin-ni-MENT) *n.* liniment
"Mus' rub wid linniment fuh
cyo' mis'ry een de j'int."
(You must rub with liniment to
cure rheumatism.)

lissut
(LIS-sut) *n.* lizzard/-s
"De cat ketch uh lissut."
(The cat caught a lizzard.)

locus
(LO-cus) *adj.* local
"Dem locus gal."

(They are local girls.)

'long
(LONG) *adv.* along; with
"De chile gone 'long 'e ma."
(The child went with his mother.)

long-cheer
(LONG-cheer) *n.* long chair; sofa
"All t'ree dem set on de long-cheer."
(All three of them sat on the sofa.)

long'mout'
(LONG-mout) *adj.* long mouth; pouting expression of the mouth
"Dat long'mout' gal oagly fuh true."
(That pouting girl is truly ugly.)

long talk
(LONG talk) *n.* idle chatter; gossip
"Long talk mek trouble."
(Gossip makes trouble.)

look lukkuh
(LOOK lukkuh) *id.* looks like; apparently
"'E look lukkuh Joe t'ief de mule."
(It looks like Joe stole the mule.)

los'
(LOS) *v.* lose/-s, lost, losing
"Eb'ry time uh g'em money, 'e los'um."
(Every time I give him money he loses it.)

'low
(LOW) *v.* allow; admit/-s/-ed/-ing
"Bubbuh 'low 'e bruk de ax."
(Brother admitted that he broke the ax.)

'low'um
(LOW-um) *v.* allow them
"De row boss ent 'low'um fuh lef' de fiel'."
(The overseer did not allow them to leave the field.)

lub
(LUB) *v.* love/-s, loved, loving
"Uh lub dat gal tummuch!"
(I love that girl very much!)

luk
(LUK) *prep.* like; comparable to
"De gal look luk 'e maamy."
(The girl looks like her mother.)

lukkuh
(LUK-KUH) *prep.* like
NOTE: SEE *LUK*. *LUKKUH* AND *LUK* ARE USED INTERCHANGEABLY.

M

maa'ch
(MAACH) *v.* march/-es/-ed/-ing
"De chillun duh maa'ch down de road; dey call demse'f

sodjuh."
(The children are marching down the road; they are pretending to be soldiers.)

Maa'ch
(MAACH) *PN.* March
"Dem git yuh een Maa'ch munt'."
(They came here in March.)

maa'k
(MAAK) *v.* mark/-s/-ed/-ing
"'E maa'k de row weh 'e lef' off."
(She marked the row where she stopped working.)

maa'k'um
(MAAK-um) *id.* marked him/her/it/them
"'E ma maa'k'um fuh frog."
(His mother's fear has caused him to look like a frog.)
NOTE: MANY GULLAH BELIEVE THAT AN EXPECTANT MOTHER'S FEAR OF AN ANIMAL OR A THING CAN CAUSE HER UNBORN CHILD TO RESEMBLE THAT WHICH SHE FEARS.

maamy
(MAA-my) *n.* mother
"Maamy laa'n me fuh weabe baskut."
(Mother taught me to weave baskets.)

maa'sh
(MAASH) *n.* marsh/-es
"Uh bog de maa'sh fuh oshtuh."
(I bogged the marshes for oysters.)

maa'sh hen
(MAASH hen) *n.* marsh hen/-s; a bird that resembles a small hen and lives in the marsh
"Bubbuh shoot 'nuf maa'sh hen."
(Brother shot many marsh hens.)

man-chillun
(MAN-chil-lun) *n.* male children; boys; sons
"Mistuh Noruh en' 'e man-chillun bil' de aa'k."
(Mister Noah and his sons built the ark.)

man-dog
(MAN-dog) *n.* male dog
"Pa hab two man-dog."
(Father has two male dogs.)

mange
(MANGE) *n.* mane
"De rope twis'up een de hawss mange."
(The rope is twisted in the horse's mane.)

mannus
(MAN-nus) *n.* good manners; politeness
"Dat boy ent hab no mannus."
(That boy is impolite.)

mannusubble
(MAN-nus-ub-ble) *adj.* courteous
"Joe mannusubble, fuh true."
(Joe is certainly polite.)

manuity
    (man-U-i-ty) *n.* manure/-s
    "Uh done tote t'ree load ub manuity dey dey."
    (I have already carried three loads of manure there.)

marriage'um
    (MAR-RIAGE-um) *id.* mix or blend it/them
    "Bruk uh aig en' marriage'um tuh de mixjuh."
    (Break an egg and blend it into the mixture.)

marri'd
    (MAR-rid) *v.* marry, marries, married, marrying
    "Dis week mek de two munt' sence dem marri'd."
    (They have been married two months this past week.)

marruh
    (MAR-ruh) *n.* marrow; brain
    "De chile ent hab ub marruh een 'e head."
    (The child doesn't have a brain in his head.)

mas'
    (MAS) *n.* master/s
    "Mas' John gi'we 'nuf gritch."
    (Master John gave us plenty of grits.)

matches
    (MAT-ches) n. match/-es
    "Pa ax fuh uh matches fuh light 'e pipe."
    (Father asked for a match to light his pipe.)

maussuh
    (MAUS-suh) *n.* master/s
    "Mistuh John Heywu'd me maussuh."
    (Mister John Heyward is my master.)

mawk'n'bu'd
    (MAWK-'n-bud) *n.* mockingbird
    "Dat mawk'n'bu'd bin sing all t'ru' de night."
    (That mockingbird has been singing all through the night.)

mawnin'
    (MAWN-in) *inter.* morning; good morning
    "Uh tell'um mawnin'."
    (I greeted them, good morning.)

med'sin
    (MED-cine) *n.* medicine/-s
    "De doctuh g'em med'sin fuh 'e teet'ache."
    (The doctor gave him medicine for his toothache.)

medjuh
    (MED-juh) *n.* measure; one cup
    "Pit uh medjuh ub molasses een de cake."
    (Put a cup of molasses in the cake.)

me
    (ME) *pron.* I; my
    "Dat me mule."
    (That's my mule.)

meet'n'
(MEET-'n) *n.* meeting; a religious service
"Sunday us gwine tuh meet'n'."
(We are going to church on Sunday.)

meet'um so
(MEET-um SO) *id.* found it in its present condition
"De boy suh 'e yent bruk de hoe, 'e meet'um so."
(The boy said he didn't break the hoe, it was already broken when he found it.)

mek
(MEK) *v.* make/-s, made, making
"Ma mek two cake."
(Mother made two cakes.)

mek'ace
(MEK-ace) *id.* make haste; move quickly
"Mek'ace en' fetch de watuh."
(Hurry and bring the water.)

mek ansuh
(MEK an-suh) *v.* make answer; reply, replies, replied, replying
"'E mek ansuh suh 'e yent do'um."
(He replied saying he didn't do it.)

mek 'e maa'k
(mek e MAAK) *id.* make his/her mark; sign/-s his/her name
"Pa mek 'e maa'k 'pun de papuh."
(Father signed the paper.)

mek 'e mannus
(mek e MAN-NUS) *v.* make his/her manners; bow or curtsy
"W'en de pastuh come, de chile mek 'e mannus."
(When the pastor came, the child bowed.)

mek 'ese'f 'ka'ce
(mek e-sef KACE) *id.* make him/herself scarce; hide/-s, hid, hiding oneself/themselves
"Mistuh Adam mek 'ese'f 'ka'ce."
(Mister Adam hid himself.)

Mek 'e yent set tuh one side?
(MEK e yent SET tuh ONE SIDE) *id.* Why doesn't he/she stay out of the way?

mek fuh
(MEK fuh) *v.* [make for]; go directly toward
"Fus' daa'k de gal mek fuh home."
(At sundown the girl went directly home.)

mek hebby complain
(mek heb-by COM-PLAIN) *id.* make heavy complaint; complain loudly
"Pa mek hebby complain w'en de wedduh tek 'e crap."
(Father complained loudly when the rain ruined his crop.)

mek 'mirashun
(mek MIR-a-shun) *v.* [made admiration]; admired
"Miss May mek 'mirashun obuh de gal frock."
(Miss May admired the girl's dress.)

mek mout' f'um yez tuh yez
(mek mout fum YEZ tuh YEZ) *id.* make mouth from ear to ear; grin broadly
"Jake mek mout' f'um yez tuh yez, 'e dat happy."
(Jake was so happy, he grinned from one ear to the other.)

mek out
(MEK out) *v.* pretend/-s/-ed/-ing
"De 'ooman mek out 'e gwine home."
(The woman pretended she was going home.)

mek so
(mek SO) *adv.* why
"Mek so de chile ent gone school?"
(Why didn't the child go to school?)

mek track fuh
(mek TRACK fuh) *id.* make tracks for; leave hurriedly for
"W'en de bell ring, uh mek track fuh de baa'n."
(When the bell rang, I hurried to the barn.)

'membuh
(MEM-buh) *v.* remember/-s/-ed/-ing
"'Membuh mus' feed de hawss."
(Remember, you must feed the horse.)

'memb'unce
(MEM-bunce) *n.* remembrance/-s; memory
"Pit flowuh 'pun Pa grabe fuh 'e 'memb'unce."
(Put flowers on Father's grave in his memory.)

men' 'e pace
(men e PACE) *id.* mend his/her/their pace; quicken the pace
"Ma tell'um mus' men' 'e pace."
(Mother told them to mend their pace.)

mese'f
(me-SEF) *pron.* myself
"Uh gwine mese'f!"
(I, myself, am going!)

mess wid
(MESS wid) *id.* mess with; bother
"Uh tell'um mus' don't mess wid dat mule."
(I told them not to bother that mule.)

metsage
(MET-sage) *n.* message/-s
"Bubbuh sen' metsage suh us mus' come home."
(Brother sent a message saying we must come home.)

middleday
(MID-DLE-day) *n.* middle of the day; noon
"W'en middleday come, 'e gone fuh plow."
(When it was noon he went to plow.)

middlenight
(MID-DLE-night) *n.* the middle of the night; midnight
"'E git home 'fo' middlenight."
(He got home before midnight.)

milk-bubbuh
(milk-BUB-BUH) *n.* milk brother/-s; children who have been nursed by the same wet nurse
"Mas' John en' Bram milk-bubbuh."
(Master John and Abraham were milk brothers.)

min' 'e mannus
(MIN e MAN-nus) *id.* mind his/her/their manners; behave properly; act politely
"Uh tell de chile mus' min' 'e mannus tuh de chu'ch."
(I told the child that she must mind her manners in church.)

mischeebus
(mis-CHEE-bus) *adj.* mischievous
"Nina leetle gal too mischeebus."
(Nina's little girl is very mischievous.)

mis'ry een 'e j'int
(MIS-RY een e jint) *n.* misery in his/her joint/-s; arthritis; rheumatism
"De ole man strick wid de mis'ry een 'e j'int."
(The old man is stricken with arthritis.)

Mistuh
(MIS-tuh) *PN.* Mister
"Mistuh Tom sell de mule."
(Mister Tom sold the mule.)

mo'
(MO) *adv.* more; to the greater degree
"Jane mo' tall dan Liza; Della tall de mores."
(Jane is taller than Liza; Della is tallest of the three.)

mock'n'bu'd
(MOCK-'n-bud) *n.* mockingbird
"De mock'n'bu'd sing sof'ly all t'ru de night."
(The mockingbird sings softly all through the night.

mo'n
(MON) *v.* mourn/-s/-ed/-ing
"'E duh mo'n fuh 'e lawfully lady."
(He is mourning for his wife.)

monkry
(MONK-ry) *n.* monkey/-s
"De mo' high de monkry climb, de mo' de chillun laugh at'um."

(The higher the monkey climbed, the more the children laughed at him.)

mo'nuh
(MO-nuh) *conj.* more than
"Uh luk rice mo'nuh hom'ny."
(I like rice more than hominy.)

moobe
(MOOBE) *v.* move/-s/-d, moving
"Dem done moobe f'um de faa'm."
(They have already moved from the farm.)

mores'
(MORES) *adv.* most; to the greatest degree
"Jane mo' tall dan Liza; Della tall de mores'."
(Jane is taller than Liza; Della is tallest of the three.)

'mos'
(MOS) *adv.* almost
"De chile 'mos' done nyam 'e bittle."
(The child has almost finished eating his food.)

mo'soonuh
(mo-SOON-uh) *adv.* [more] sooner
"Ef 'e lef' mo'soonuh, 'e could'uh ketch de strain."
(If he had left sooner, he could have caught the train.)

mout'
(MOUT) *n.* mouth/-s
"'E mout' stan' f'um yez tuh yez."
(His mouth seems to reach from one of his ears to the other.)

mout' box-up
(MOUT BOX-up) *id.* a surly expression, accomplished by closing the mouth and drawing it down at the corners
"Ma is too bex, 'e mout' box-up."
(Mother is so vexed, her mouth has a surly expression.)

mout' dry-up
(MOUT dry-up) *adj.* speechless
"De boy skay'd 'tel 'e mout' dry-up."
(The boy is so scared, he is unable to talk.)

mout' duh leak
(MOUT duh LEAK) *id.* the mouth is leaking; salivate/-s/-ed/-ing
"De dog so hongry 'e mout' duh leak."
(The dog is so hungry he is salivating.)

muffle-jaw
(MUF-FLE-jaw) *n.* a variety of chicken, characterized by feathers around the face suggestive of a muffler
"Ma gwi' set de muffle-jaw fuh 'e hab biddy."
(Mother is going to let the muffle-jaw brood to have

mukkul
(MUK-KUL) *n.* myrtle tree
"De redbu'd mek 'e nes' een de mukkul."
(The redbird made his nest in the myrtle tree.)

munt'
(MUNT) *n.* month/-s
"De gal lef' een Augus' munt'."
(The girl left in August.)
NOTE: THE WORD *MUNT'* ALWAYS FOLLOWS THE NAME OF THE MONTH.

murruh
(MUR-ruh) *n.* mother/s
"Murruh done fuh dead."
(Mother has been dead for a long time.)
NOTE: THIS IS A TERM SELDOM HEARD TODAY, EXCEPT IN THE SPEECH OF OLDER GULLAH PEOPLE.

mus' don'
(MUS DON) *id.* must not
"Mus' don' fly een Gawd face."
(You must not question the wisdom of God.)

mus'e
(MUS-e) *id.* must be
"Oonuh mus'e racktify een 'e min'."
(You must be crazy.)

muskick
(MUS-kick) *n.* musket/-s
"Grumpa suh de sodjuh tote muskick."
(Grandfather said the soldiers carried muskets.)

muskittuh
(mus-KITT-uh) n. mosquito/-es
"Muskittuh mek we eetch."
(The mosquitoes made us itch.)

mussy
(MUSS-y) *n.* mercy
"Lawd hab mussy!"
(Lord have mercy!)

N

naby
(NA-by) *n.* navy
"Uh gwi' jine de naby."
(I'm going to join the navy.)

nakity
(NA-kit-y) *adj.* naked
"Dem po' 'tel dey nakity."
(They don't have clothes to wear, they're so poor.)

natchul
(NAT-chul) *adv.* [natural]; truly
"De natchul hongry hab'um."
(They are truly hungry.)

navuh
(NA-vuh) *n.* neighbor/-s
"Sistuh gone tuh 'e navuh house."
(Sister has gone to her neighbor's house.)

Nawt'
(NAWT) *PN.* North
"Sam dem come f'um de Nawt'."
(Sam and the others came from the North.)

nebbuh
(NEB-buh) *adv.* never
"Porgy ent nebbuh come back."
(Porgy never came back.)

nebbuh count'um
(NEG-buh COUNT-um) *id.* completely disregard someone or something
"Maria juntleman nebbuh count'um."
(Maria's husband pays no attention to her.)

needuh
(NEED-uh) *adj.* neither
"Needuh one hab shoesh."
(Neither one has shoes.)

needuh'so
(NEED-uh-so) *conj.* nor
"John needuh'so Mary jine de chu'ch."
(Neither John nor Mary joined the church.)

'neet'
(NEET) *adv.* beneath; underneath
"De chickin gone 'neet' de house."
(The chickens have gone underneath the house.)
NOTE: *'NEET'* AND *ONDUHNEET'* ARE USED INTERCHANGEABLY.

nemmine
(NEM-mine) *id.* never mind; do not be concerned
"Nemmine; 'e yent know wuh 'e duh talk 'bout."
(Don't be concerned; he doesn't know what he is talking about.)

new bran'
(NEW BRAN) *adj.* brand new
"Ella hab on new bran' shoesh."
(Ella is wearing brand new shoes.)

newfangledy
(NEW-FAN-GLE-dy) *adj.* newfangled; fashionable
"De shoesh berry newfangledy."
(The shoes are very fashionable.)

new groun'
(NEW groun) *n.* new ground; soil that has never been planted
"Pa gone fuh plow de new groun'."
(Father has gone to plow the field that has never been planted.)

Newnited State
(NEW-nit-ed STATE) *PN.* United States
"Us lib duh de Newnited State."
(We live in the United States.)

nice'um'up
(NICE-um-up) *id.* flatter/-s/

-ed/-ing him/her/them
"Uh nice'um'up fuh 'e gimme candy."
(I flattered her so she would give me candy.)

niece
(NIECE) *n.* niece or nephew
"Mary en' John alltwo 'e niece."
(Mary and John are his nieces.)
NOTE: THE WORD NEPHEW IS NOT USED BY THE GULLAH PEOPLE.

nigh'um
(NIGH-um) *adv.* nigh/near him/her/it/them
"W'en de dog nigh'um, 'e run."
(When the dog was near him, he ran.)

no
(NO) *adj.* any
"Us ent hab no money."
(We don't have any money.)

no'mannus
(NO-man-nus) *adj.* [no manners]; impolite
"Della chillun berry no'mannus."
(Della's children are very impolite.)

Noruh
(NO-ruh) *PN.* Noah
"Mistuh Noruh en' 'e manchillun bil' de aa'k."
(Mister Noah and his sons built the art.)

nott
(NOTT) *n.* nut/-s
"Pit uh medjuh ub nott een de cake."
(Put a cup of nuts in the cake.)

notus
(NO-tus) *v.* notice/-s/-ed/-ing; tend
"Notus de baby!"
(Tend the baby!)

Nowembuh
(NO-wem-buh) *PN.* November
"Punkin ripe een Nowembuh munt'."
(Pumpkins are ripe in November.)

'nuf
(NUF) *adj.* enough; plenty; many
"Us hab 'nuf bittle."
(We have plenty of food.)

'Nuffuh wu'd eat-up wuh dey duh talk 'bout.
(nuf-fuh wud EAT-UP wuh dey duh TALK BOUT) *id.* Too much discussion is disconcerting.

nuh
(NUH) *conj.* nor
"'E nuh me t'ief de candy."
(Neither he nor I took the candy.)

nuss
(NUSS) *n.* nurse/-s
"De chile nuss gone 'long'um."
(The child's nurse went with her.)

nutt'n'
(NUTT-'n) *n.* nothing
"Nutt'n' ail'um!"
(There's nothing wrong with him!)

nyam
(NYAM) *v.* eat/-s, ate, eating
"'E nyam 'e bittle."
(He ate his food.)

nyankee
(NYANK-ee) *adj.* yankee
"Dat nyankee gal berry swonguh."
(That yankee girl is very boastful.)

nyung
(NYUNG) *adj.* young
"Nyung gal berry lub fuh dance."
(Young girls like very much to dance.)

nyuse
(NYUSE) *v.* use/-s/-ed/-ing
"'E nyuse tuh lib' yuh."
(He used to live here.)

O

oagly
(OAG-ly) *adj.* ugly
"Dat dog too oagly."
(That dog is very ugly.)

ob'shay
(OB-SHAY) *n.* overseer/-s
"De ob'shay berry no'mannus."
(The overseer is very rude.)

obuh
(OB-UH) *prep.* over
"T'row de ball obuh de house."
(Throw the ball over the house.)

Octobuh
(oc-TOB-uh) *PN.* October
"De fus' fros' come een Octobuh munt'."
(The first frost came in october.)

odduh
(ODD-uh) *adj.* other
"De odduh chillun bin fight."
(The other children were fighting.)

odduh'res'
(od-duh-RES) *adj.* the others; the rest
"De odduh'res' gone home."
(The rest of the children went home.)

offuhr'um
(OF-FUH-rum) *id.* offer/-s/-ed/-ing him/her/it/them
"Ma offuhr'um some pie."
(Mother offered them some pie.)

ole
(OLE) *adj.* old
"De ole 'ooman berry sick."
(The old woman is very sick.)

oncommun
(ON-com-mon) *adv.* uncommonly; unusually
"'E oncommun lazy en' no-

count."
(He is unusually lazy and worthless.)

ondeestunt
(on-DEE-stunt) *adj.* indecent
"De police 'res'um bekase 'e clothes ondeestunt."
(The police arrested him because his clothes were indecent.)

onduhneet'
(ON-duh-NEAT) *adv.* underneath
"Pa duh set onduhneet' de tree."
(Father is sitting underneath the tree.)

onduhstan'
(ON-duh-STAN) *v.* understand/-s, understood, understanding
"De leetle gal ent onduhstan' huffuh read."
(The little girl does not understand how to read.)

onduhtekuh
(ON-duh-TEK-uh) *n.* undertaker/-s
"'E dead en' de onduhtekuh hab' 'e body."
(He is dead and the undertaker has his body.)

one
(ONE) *adj.* alone; only
"Gawd, one, kin do'um."
(God, alone, can do it.)

one'nudduh
(one-NUD-DUH) *n.* one another
"Dey duh fau't one'nudduh."
(They are criticizing one another.)

onhitch
(ON-HITCH) *v.* unhitch; divorce
"Joe en' Della pay t'irty dolluh fuh git onhitch."
(Joe and Della paid thirty dollars for a divorce.)

onkibbuh
(on-KIB-BUH) *v.* uncover
"'E onkibbuh 'e yeye fuh see wuh eb'rybody duh do."
(He uncovered his eyes to see what everybody was doing.)

onmannussubble
(on-MAN-NUSS-ub-ble) *adj.* without manners; impolite
"'E too unmannussubble en' lazy."
(He is too impolite and lazy.)

onrabble
(on-RAB-BLE) *v.* unravel; untangle
"Onrabble de fishline."
(Untangle the fishing line.)

onrabble 'e mout'
(on-RAB-BLE e MOUT) *id.* unravel the mouth; ramble or talk at great length; gossip
"De 'ooman unrabble 'e mout' 'bout de paa'ty."
(The women talked at length about the party.)

onsutt'n
(on-SAA-t'n) *adj.* uncertain
"'E onsaa't'n w'en de chile been bawn."
(She was uncertain when the child was born.)

onsattify
(on-SATT-i-fy) *v.* unsatisfied
"Miss Ebe onsattify; 'e bound' fuh tas'e de apple."
(Miss Eve was unsatisfied; she was bound to taste the apple.)

ontel
(on-TEL) *adv.* until
"Uh gwi' set yuh ontel fus' daa'k."
(I am going to sit here until the sun goes down.)
NOTE: *ONTEL* AND *'TEL* ARE USED INTERCHANGEABLY.

'ood
(OOD) *n.* wood, woods
"Den uh gwine duh 'ood."
(Then I'm going into the woods.)

'ooman
(OO-man) *n.* woman, women
"T'ree 'ooman bin duh de sto'."
(Three women were at the store.)

oonuh
(OO-nuh) *pron.* you
"Oonuh shum?"
(Did you see them?)

Oonuh hab 'e name?
(OO-nuh hab e NAME) *id.*
Do you have your calling card?

Oonuh hab sweet toot'?
(OO-nuh hab SWEET toot) *id.*
Do you want something sweet to eat?

oshtuh
(OSH-tuh) *n.* oyster/-s
"Uh bog de maa'sh fuh oshtuh."
(I bogged the marsh for oysters.)

out
(OUT) *v.* outen/-s/-ed/-ing; extinguish/-s/-ed/-ing
"Out de fiah!"
(Extinguish the fire!)

owbry
(OW-bry) *n.* eyebrow/-s
"'E owbry t'ick."
(His eyebrows are thick.)

P

paa'd'n
(PAA-d'n) *n.* pardon
"De Maussuh g'em paa'd'n."
(The Master gave him pardon.)

paa'd'n
(PAA-d'n) *v.* pardon/-s/-ed/-ing
"De Maussuh paa'd'n'um."
(The Master pardoned him.)

paa'luh
(PAA-luh) *n.* parlor/-s
(Saa'b de tea een de paa'luh.)

(Serve the tea in the parlor.)

paa's'n
(PAA-s'n) *n.* parson/-s
"De paa's'n preach 'bout Mistuh Noruh en' de aa'k."
(The parson preached about Mister Noah and the ark.)

paat'
(PAAT) *n.* path/s
"Dem peruse 'long de paat' 'fo' dem paa't."
(They walked slowly along the path before they parted.)

paa't
(PAAT) *n.* part/-s
"Paa't de con'regation een de chu'ch."
(Part of the congregation is in the church.)

paa'ty
(PAA-ty) *n.* party, parties
"All de chillun dem gone tuh de paa'ty."
(All of the children they have gone to the party.)

papuh
(PA-puh) *n.* paper/-s; a written agreement
"Papuh 'pun'top de house."
(There is a written agreement concerning the house.)

par'sipate
(PAR-si-pate) *v.* participate
"No mattuh wuh you duh do, dem chillun ent gwi' par'sipate."
(No matter what you do, those children are not going to participate.)

parrysawl
(PAR-RY-sawl) *n.* parasol/-s
"De lady hab parrysawl so de sunhot cyan' bu'n'um."
(The lady has a parasol so the heat of the sun can't burn her.)

pashun
(PASH-un) *n.* patience
"Uh too bex; uh yent hab no mo' pashun wid'um."
(I'm too angry; I don't have any more patience with them.)

pastuh
(PAS-tuh) *n.* pastor/-s
"De pastuh lef' 'e hat tuh de chu'ch."
(The pastor left his hat at the church.)

pastuh
(PAS-tuh) *n.* pasture/-s
"Fibe hawss bin een de pastuh."
(Five horses were in the pasture.)

patty-rolluh
(pat-ty-ROLL-uh) *n.* patroler; policeman
"De t'ief graff de bag en' gone 'fo' de patty-rolluh ketch'um."
(The thief grabbed the bag and left before the policeman caught him.)

'paw'tun'
 (PAW-tun) *adj.* importance
 "De Prezzydent uh berry
 'paw'tun' puss'n."
 (The President is a very
 important person.)

peaceubble
 (PEACE-ub-ble) *adj.* peaceful
 "Dat ole bull stan' berry
 peaceubble 'tell sump'n'
 bex'um."
 (That old bull is very peaceful
 until something vexes him.)

'pen'pun
 (pen-PUN) *v.* depend/-s upon
 "Ef us gwine de picnic
 'pen'pun de wedduh."
 (Whether or not we go to the
 picnic depends upon the
 weather.)

peruse
 (pe-RUSE) *v.* walk slowly, or
 aimlessly
 "Ma tell Bubbuh mus'
 mek'ace, 'cep' 'e yent
 pay'um no min'; 'e peruse."
 (Mother told Brother to hurry,
 but he paid no attention; he
 walked slowly.)

piggin
 (PIG-gin) *n.* bucket/-s
 "Tek de piggin en' fetch de
 watuh."
 (Take the bucket and bring the
 water.)

pinch'um
 (PINCH-um) *id.* [pinch/-es
 him/her]; an expression of
 discomfort
 "'E belly pinch'um."
 (He is hungry.)

p'int
 (PINT) *n.* point/-s
 "De pen p'int bruk."
 (The pen point is broken.)

p'int
 (PINT) *v.* point/-s/-ed/-ing
 "'E duh p'int tuh de sto'."
 (He is pointing to the store.)

'p'int
 (PINT) *v.* appoint/-s/-ed/-ing
 "'E 'p'int fuh saa'b two yeah."
 (He was apointed to serve two
 years.)

'Piskubble
 (pis-KIB-BLE) *PN.* Episcopal
 "Dem gone de 'Piskubble
 Chu'ch."
 (They went to the Episcopal
 Church.)

pit
 (PIT) *v.* put
 "Pit de chickin een de pot."
 (Put the chicken in the pot.)

p'izen
 (PI-zen) *n.* poison/-s
 "De p'izen mek 'e laig swell."
 (The poison made his leg
 swell.)

plantesshun
 (plan-TES-shun) *n.* plantation/
 -s
 "Two new han' come tuh de
 plantesshun."

(Two new workers [field hands] came to the plantation.)

'plash
(PLASH) *v.* splash/-s/-ed/-ing
"De mud 'plash all obuh 'e shoesh."
(The mud splashed all over his shoes.)

plateye
(PLAT-eye) n. a ghost whose shining eyes terrify the beholder
"Uh shum de plateye duh de 'ood een Jedgetown."
(I saw the plateye in the woods in Georgetown.)

please kin
(PLEASE kin) *id.* please [can], may
"Please kin Uh hab some candy?"
(May I have some candy, please?)

pledjuh
(PLED-juh) *v.* enjoy
"De Lawd tell Miss Ebe mus' pledjuh 'ese'f een de Gyaa'd'n."
(The Lord told Miss Eve to enjoy herself in the Garden.)

po'
(PO) *adj.* poor
"Dat lan' mek berry po' crap."
(That land makes very poor crops.)

po'
(PO) v. pour/-s/-ed/-ing

"'E duh po' de watuh een de pot."
(She is pouring the water in the pot.)

po' creetuh
(po CREE-tuh) *n.* a sick or mistreated animal
"Dat po' creetuh too hongry."
(That poor creature is very hungry.)

po'ch
(POCH) *n.* porch/-es
"Ma dey dey de po'ch, duh set een 'e rockuh cheer."
(Mother is right there on the porch, sitting in her rocking chair.)

po'ly
(PO-ly) *adj.* poorly; not in good health
"His he'lt' sawtuh po'ly."
(His health is [sort of] poor.)

'posit 'e wu'd
(POS-it e wud) *id.* give his/her word; swear to
"Pa done 'posit 'e wu'd."
(Father has sworn to it.)

positubble
(POS-it-ub-ble) *adv.* positively
"'E tell we positubble 'e gwi' do'um."
(He told us positively that he is going to do it.)

pot likkuh
(POT li-quo) *n.* pot liquor; the liquid in cooked vegetables
"Sabe de pot likkuh fuh nyam

'long de rice."
(Save the pot liquor to eat with the rice.)

pot salt
(POT salt) *n.* table salt
"Pit 'nuf pot salt een'um."
(Season it well with salt.)

pot spoon
(POT spoon) *n.* a large spoon used to stir the pot during cooking
"Mus' don' eat wid de pot spoon."
(Don't eat with the spoon you used to stir the pot.)

praise-meet'n'
(PRAISE-meet-'n) *n.* prayer meeting
"Eb'ry We'n'sd'y Ma gone praise-meet'n'."
(Every Wednesday Mother goes to prayer meeting.)

'prentus han'
(PREN-tus HAN) *n.* [apprentice hand]; a helper
"Uh berry glad fuh 'prentus han'."
(I'm very glad to have a helper.)

projic'
(PROJ-ic) *v.* interfere
"'E come fuh projic' wid me bidness."
(He came to interfere with my business.)

proobe
(PROOBE) *v.* prove/-s/-ed-/ing

"'E cyan' proobe de hawss duh him'own."
(He can't prove that the horse is his.)

puhtek
(puh-TEK) *v.* protect/-s/-ed/-ing
"Bubbuh hab uh dog fuh puhtek 'e house."
(Brother has a dog to protect his house.)

puhwide
(puh-WIDE) *v.* provide/-s/-ed/-ing
"Pa haffuh wu'k haa'd fuh puhwide fuh 'e chillun."
(Father has to work hard to provide for his children.)

puhzac'ly
(puh-ZAC-ly) *adv.* exactly
"Uh yent know puhzac'ly weh 'e gone."
(I don't know exactly where he went.)

punkin-skin
(PUNK-in-skin) *id.* "punkin" describes the skin color of a mulatto
"Dat punkin-skin gal done gone back tuh towng."
(That mulatto girl has gone back to town.)

punshun
(PUN-shun) *n.* puncheon/-s; split logs
"De swamp road mek ub punshun."
(The swamp road is made of

split logs.)

'pun'top
 (pun-TOP) *adv.* upon the top; on top; upon
 "De cat 'pun'top de house."
 (The cat is on top of the house.)

puss'n
 (PUSS-'n) *n.* person/-s
 "Twelbe puss'n bin bactize."
 (Twelve persons were baptized.)

pyo'
 (PYO) *adj.* pure
 "Dey ent hab nutt'n' fuh eat 'cep' de pyo' cawn hom'ny."
 (They don't have anything to eat except plain hominy.)

pyo'-ack
 (PYO-ack) *id.* pure act; pretense
 "Dat gal ent sick; dat de pyo'-ack."
 (That girl isn't sick; that is an act.)

Q

'quaintun'
 (QUAIN-tun) *v.* acquainted
 "Uh bin 'quaintun' wid alltwo de gal."
 (I was acquainted with both girls.)

quality-buckruh
 (qual-i-ty-BUCK-ruh) *id.* well-to-do, influential white people
 "Me maussuh bin quality-buckruh."
 (My master was a well-to-do white man.)

quawl
 (QUAWL) *v.* quarrel/-s/-ed/-ing
 "De two 'ooman quawl 'bout de hen."
 (The two women quarreled about the hen.)

quawt
 (QUAWT) *n.* quart/-s
 "De cow gib fibe quawt ub milk."
 (The cow gave five quarts of milk.)

'queeze
 (QUEEZE) *v.* squeeze/-s/-ed/-ing
 "Pa 'queeze de grape fuh mek wine."
 (Father squeezed the grapes to make wine.)

quile
 (QUILE) *n.* coil/-s
 "De fiah sen' smoke quile up de chimbly."
 (The fire sent smoke coils up the chimney.)

'quire
 (QUIRE) *v.* inquire; require; acquire
 "Uh 'quire 'bout'um, 'cep'm 'e yent dey."
 (I inquired about him but he was not there.)

quizzit
(QUIZ-zit) *v.* question/-s/-ed/-ing; ask/-s/-ed/-ing
"Den Uh quizzit 'e fam'bly."
(Then I questioned his family.)

R

racktify
(RACK-ti-fy) *adj.* broken; no longer useful
"De cyaa't so ole 'e racktify."
(The cart is so old it's of no more use.)

ramify 'roun'
(RAM-i-fy) *id.* act like a ram; behave rudely or unmannerly
"Dat no'mannus man duh ramify 'roun'."
(That unmannerly man acts very rude.)

rappit
(RAP-pit) *adv.* [rapid]; rapidly; quickly
"Dey quizzit me rappit."
(They questioned me rapidly.)

rayre
(RAYRE) *v.* rear/-s/-ed/-ing
"De hawss rayre en' t'row'um."
(The horse reared and threw him.)

recishun
(re-CI-shun) *n.* decision/-s
"Uh done mek recishun fuh j'ine de chu'ch."
(I have made the decision to join the church.)

reb'ren'
(REB-ren) *n.* reverend/-s
"De reb'ren' bactize all ub we."
(The reverend baptized all of us.)

redduh
(RED-duh) *adv.* rather
"Uh redduh stay yuh."
(I would rather stay here.)

refen'
(re-FEN) *v.* defend/-s/-ed/-ing
"Bubbuh jine de aa'my fuh refen' 'e country."
(Brother joined the army to defend his country.)

remonia
(re-MON-ia) *n.* pneumonia
"De doctuh suh de chile hab de remonia."
(The doctor said the child has pneumonia.)

renite
(re-NITE) *v.* unite/-s/-ed/-ing; reunite/-s/-ed/-ing
"All ub we gwi' renite nex' Chuesday."
(We will have a reunion next Tuesday.)

repeah
(re-PE-AH) *v.* appear/-s/-ed/-ing
"De ainjul repeah tuh Mary."
(The angel appeared to Mary.)

resplain
(res-PLAIN) *v.* explain/-s/-ed/-ing

"Ma resplain how de baskut mek."
(Mother explained how the basket was made.)

ribbuh
(RIB-BUH) *n.* river/-s
"'Nuf fish dey een de ribbuh."
(Plenty of fish are there in the river.)

ride 'e frame
(RIDE e FRAME) *id.* [ride his/her frame]; fight him/her
"Uh ride 'e frame 'tell dat man drap."
(I fought that man until he dropped.)

roas'n' yeah
(ROAS-'n YEAH) *n.* ripe corn
"De roas'n' yeah ready fuh nyam."
(The ripe corn is ready to eat.)

rokkoon
(ROK-koon) *n.* raccoon/-s
"Rokkoon berry good fuh nyam 'long sweet tettuh."
(Raccoon is very good to eat with sweet potato.)
NOTE: THE WORD *COON* IS ALSO USED.

rozzum tree
(ROZ-zum tree) *n.* [rosin tree]; pine tree
"Rozzum tree splintuh stan' berry good fuh mek fiah."
(Pine tree splinters are very good to make a fire.)

ruckuhnize
(RUCK-uh-NIZE) *v.* recognize/-s/-ed-ing
"Uh yent shum fuh so long, uh mos' ent ruckuhnize'um."
(I haven't seen them for so long, I almost didn't recognize them.)

rumpletail
(RUMP-le-TAIL) *n.* a rooster that has lost his tail feathers
"Dat de ole rumpletail duh crow."
(That is the old tailless rooster crowing.)

S

saa'b
(SAAB) *v.* serve/-s/-ed/-ing
"Mek oonuh yent saa'b de dinnuh?"
(Why don't you serve the dinner?)

saa'bint
(SAA-bint) *n.* servant/-s
"Twelbe saa'bint bin dey."
(Twelve servants were there.)

saa'bis
(SAA-bis) *n.* service/-s
"T'ree saa'bis bin hol' tuh de chu'ch."
(Three services were held at the church.)

saa'ch
(SAACH) *v.* search/-es/-ed/-ing
"All ub we bin saa'ch fuh de

t'ief."
(All of us were searching for the thief.)

saa'deen
(SAA-deen) *n.* sardine/-s
"Us hab saa'deen en' hom'ny fuh we suppuh."
(We had sardines and hominy for our supper.)

saa'pint
(SAA-pint) *n.* serpent/-s
"De saa'pint hol' cumpuhsayshun 'long Miss Ebe."
(The serpent held a conversation with Miss Eve.)

sabe
(SABE) *v.* save/-s/-ed/-ing
"Ma duh save de chickin fedduh fuh mek pilluh."
(Mother is saving the chicken feathers to make pillows.)

salary
(SAL-e-ry) *n.* celery
"De salery cos' seb'nty cent."
(The celery costs seventy cents.)

same fashi'n
(same FASH-'n) *id.* in the same manner
"De two gal walk same fashi'n."
(The two girls walk the same way.)

same lukkuh
(same LUK-kuh) *id.* just like
"'E look same lukkuh 'e ma."
(He looks just like his mother.)

Sandy Claw
(san-dy CLAW) *PN.* Santa Claus
"Uh skay'd ub Sandy Claw."
(I'm afraid of Santa Claus.)

Sat'd'y
(Sat-d'y) PN. Saturday
"Dem git pay Sat'd'y."
(They receive their wages on Saturday.)
NOTE: ALSO HEARD IS SAT'DAY AND SATIDDY.

Sattifackshun run 'roun' 'e mout'.
(sat-ti-FACK-shun run roun e MOUT) *id.* He/she is smiling with satisfaction [or pleasure].

sawtuh
(SAW-tuh) *adv.* sort of
"'E he'lt' sawtuh po'ly."
(His health is sort of poor.)

scrabble
(SCRAB-ble) *v.* scramble
"Scrabble t'ree aig."
(Scramble three eggs.)
"De chillun scrabble up de hill."
(The children scrambled up the hill.)

'scusin'
(SCUS-in) *prep.* [excusing]; except
"Pa wu'k eb'ry day 'scusin' Sunday."
(Father works every day except

Sunday.)

seaz'nin'
(SEAZ-nin) *n.* seasoning
"Pit 'nuf seaz'nin' een de soup."
(Put plenty of seasoning in the soup.)

seb'n
(SEB-'n) *adj.* seven
"De chile seb'n yeah ole."
(The child is seven years old.)

seb'nteen
(seb-'n-TEEN) *adj.* seventeen
"De gal een 'e seb'nteen yeah."
(The girl is in her seventeenth year.)

seb'nty
(SEB-'N-ty) *adj.* seventy
"De ole man done seb'nty."
(The old man is seventy years old.)

sedate
(se-DATE) *adv.* slowly; quietly
"De gal walk 'long de paat' berry sedate."
(The girls walked along the path very slowly.)

seddown
(sed-DOWN) *v.* sit down
"Uh yent hab time fuh seddown much."
(I seldom have time to sit down.)

'se'f
(SEF) *pron.* her/him/itself
"Tom 'se'f do'um."
(Tom did it himself.)
NOTE: *'SE'F* AND *'ESE'F* ARE USED INTERCHANGEABLY.

sen' ansuh
(sen AN-SUH) *id.* [send an answer]; send a message
"Ma sen' ansuh tuh de teachuh."
(Mother sent a message to the teacher.)

sence
(SENCE) *adv.* since
"Uh yent shum sence Augus' munt'."
(I haven't seen them since August.)

set
(SET) *v.* sit/-s, sat, sitting
"Jake duh set dey 'neet' de tree."
(Jake is sitting there underneath the tree.)

settle-'ooman
(SET-tle-oo-man) *id.* a settled woman; a middle-aged woman
"Settle-'ooman mek berry good wife."
(A settled woman makes a very good wife.)

sett'n'up
(sett-'n-UP) *n.* a wake
"'Nuf people been tuh Buh Joe sett'n'up."
(Many people were at Brother Joe's wake.)

shaa'k
(SHAAK) *n.* shark/-s
"De shaa'k so big, 'e bruk de line."
(The shark was so big, he broke the line.)

shaa'p
(SHAAP) *adj.* sharp
"Dem shaa'k hab shaa'p teet'."
(Those sharks have sharp teeth.)

shabe
(SHABE) *v.* shave/-s/-ed/-ing
"Bubbuh shabe de mule tail fuh 'e stan' stylish."
(Brother shaved the mule's tail so he would look stylish.)

shadduh
(SHAD-duh) *n.* shadow/-s
"Gawd t'row Him shadduh obuh de eart'."
(God threw His shadow over the earth.)
NOTE: THIS EXAMPLE IS AN IDIOMATIC EXPRESSION MEANING "THE SUN WENT DOWN."

she'own
(SHE-own) *pron.* hers
"Bina tell we de chickin bin she'own."
(Bina told us the chicken was hers.)

shet
(SHET) *v.* shut/s/ing
"Shet de do'."
(Shut the door.)

shimmy
(SHIM-my) *n.* chemise; petticoat
"Della pit staa'ch een 'e shimmy."
(Della put starch in her petticoat.)

shishuh
(SHISH-uh) *id.* such a
"Uh nebbuh yeddy shishuh t'ing."
(I never heard such a thing.)

sho'
(SHO) *n.* seashore
"De chillun bin tuh de sho'."
(The children went to the seashore.)

sho'
(SHO) *adv.* surely
"Uh sho' ent wan' yeddy 'bout'um."
(I surely don't want to hear about it.)

show out
(SHO-out) *v.* misbehave
"Mary spile chile show out tuh de chu'ch."
(Mary's spoiled child misbehaved at the church.)

shoesh
(SHOESH) *n.* shoe/-s
"Uh buy new Eastuh shoesh."
(I bought new Easter shoes.)

shout
(SHOUT) *n.* a religious ceremony where participants shuffle the feet while

clapping and singing

shub
(SHUB) *v.* shove/-s/-ed/-ing; push/-es/-ed/-ing
"Us haffuh shub de cyaa' fuh staa't'um."
(We had to push the car to start it.)

shum
(SHUM) *id.* see, saw, seeing him/her/it/them
"Uh shum; Uh yent yeddy'um."
(I saw them; I didn't hear them.)

shu't
(SHUT) *n.* shirt/-s
"Uh tayre me shu't."
(I tore my shirt.)

skay'd
(SKAYD) *adj.* scared; afraid
"Uh skay'd fuh true w'en Uh yeddy de t'unduh."
(Truly I was scared when I heard the thunder.)

skay-to-de't'
(SKAY-to-DET) *adj.* scared to death
"De chillun, dem, mos' skay-to-de't'."
(The children were almost scared to death.)

'skeetuh
(SKEE-tuh) *n.* mosquito/-s
"Uh mek fiah fuh de smoke run de 'skeetuh 'way."
(We made a fire so the smoke would run the mosquito away.)
NOTE: *'SKEETUH* AND *MUSKITTUH* ARE USED INTERCHANGEABLY.

sku't
(SKUT) *n.* skirt/-s
"Uh wan' de sku't scallop same fashi'n."
(I want the shirt scalloped the same way.)

slabe
(SLABE) *n.* slave/-s
"Gramma suh 'e maussuh hab seb'nty-fibe slabe."
(Grandmother said her master had seventy-five slaves.)

slam
(SLAM) *adv.* all the way
"Pa gone slam tuh towng."
(Father went all the way to town.)

slash
(SLASH) *n.* a shallow gully where water runs across a road
"W'en us git tuh de slash, de hawss ent wan' cross'um."
(When we got to the gully in the road, the horse didn't want to cross it.)

smaa't
(SMAAT) *adj.* smart
"Some dem been smaa't mo'nuh de odduh'res'."
(Some of them were smarter than the others.)

smood
(SMOOD) *adj.* smooth
"I'on de clothes 'tell dem smood."
(Iron the clothes until they are smooth.)

sode
(SWOD) *n.* sword/-s
"Gramma suh de sodjuh hab uh shaa'p sode."
(Grandmother said the soldier had a sharp sword.)

soon-man
(SOON-man) *id.* a smart, rich, or stylish man
"'Liguh binnuh soon-man f'um Sabannah."
(Elijah was a wealthy man from Savannah.)

soople 'e foot
(SOO-PLE e foot) *id.* stretch the legs
"Buh Rabbit soople 'e foot en' lean fuh de bresh."
(Brother Rabbit stretched his legs and ran toward the bushes.)

spang
(SPANG) *adv.* quickly
"Uh gone spang Chaa'stun."
(I went to Charleston as quickly as I could.)

sparrygrass
(SPAR-RY-grass) *n.* sparrowgrass; asparagus
"De chillun fin' 'nuf sparrygrass duh de ditch bank."
(The children found plenty of asparagus on the ditch bank.)

specify
(SPEC-I-FY) *v.* perform/-s/-ed/-ing; work/-s/-ed/-ing properly
"Ef de pump cyan' specify, 'e yent wu't."
(If the pump isn't working properly, it's worthless.)

speckly
(SPECK-ly) *adj.* speckled
"Dat speckly hen ent lay no aig."
(That speckled hen hasn't laid an egg.)

'spectubble
(SPECT-ub-ble) *adj.* respectable
"All dem chillun berry 'spectubble."
(All of their children are very respectable.)

sperrit
(SPER-it) *n.* spirit/-s; ghost/-s
"De ole people b'leebe sperit walk de nighttime."
(The old people believe that ghosts walk at night.)

sperritual
(SPER-it-u-al) *n.* spiritual/-s; religious song/-s
"Attuh dem done shout, Sistuh sing uh speritual."
(After they had shouted, Sister sang a religious song.)

spiduh
(SPI-duh) *n.* a large iron cooking pot
"Ma bile de hom'ny een de spiduh."
(Mother boiled the hominy in a large iron pot.)

spile
(SPILE) *v.* spoil/-s/-ed/-ing
"Dat meat done spile."
(That meat has already spoiled.)

spile 'e carricktuh
(SPILE e CAR-rick-tuh) id. spoil/-s/-ed his/her character; ruin/-s/-ed his/her reputation
"Sonny t'ief chickin en' spile 'e carricktuh."
(Sonny stole chickens and spoiled his character.)

'spishus
(SPI-shus) *adj.* suspicious
"De ole dog stan' berry 'spishus w'en de chickin dead."
(The old dog appeared very suspicious when the chicken died.)

'splain
(SPLAIN) *v.* explain/-s/-ed/-ing
"De paa's'n 'splain de Lawd wu'd."
(The parson explained the Lord's word.)

'spon'
(SPON) *v.* respond/-s/-ed/-ing
"Uh 'spon' dat Uh yent know'um."
(I responded that I didn't know them.)

'sponsubble
(SPON-sub-ble) *adv.* responsibly; also, positively
"Ma tell'um 'sponsubble mus' min' de chile."
(Mother told her positively to take care of the child.)

'spute
(SPUTE) *n.* dispute/-s
"De pastuh en' de elduh aa'bitrate de 'spute."
(The pastor and the elders settled the dispute.)

squeschun
(SQUES-chun) *n.* question/-s
"De teachuh ax tummuch squeschun."
(The teacher asks too many questions.)

staa'ch
(STAACH) *n.* starch
"Ma pit tummuch staa'ch een de clothes."
(Mother put too much starch in the clothes.)

staa'ch
(STAACH) *v.* starch/-es/-ed/-ing
"Staa'ch de clothes fuh dem i'on smood."
(Starch the clothes so that they will iron smoothly.)

staa't
(STAAT) *v.* start/-s/-ed/-ing

"'E staa't tuh wu'k 'fo' 'e git sick."
(He started to work before he got sick.)

staa't nakity
(STAAT-na-ked) *adv.* stark naked
"De baby come out de house staa't nakity."
(The baby came out of the house without any clothes on.)

stan'
(STAN) *v.* [stand]; is; appears to be
"'E he'lt' stan' berry po'."
(His health is very poor.)

stidduh
(STID-duh) *prep.* instead of
"Dem gone stidduh me."
(They went instead of me.)

stiff
(STIFF) *adj.* impertinent; saucy
"Dem chillun too stiff."
(Those children are very impertinent.)

stillyet
(still-YET) *conj.* still; yet
"Dem ent git eenbite, stillyet dey gwine dat paa'ty."
(They were not invited, still they are going to that party.)

sto'
(STO) *n.* store/-s
"'E gone sto' fuh han' t'read."
(She went to the store for sewing thread.)

'stonish
(STON-ish) *v.* astonish/-es/-ed/-ing
"W'en uh yeddy 'bout de acksident, uh been 'stonish."
(When I heard about the accident, I was astonished.)

straight'n fuh
(STRAIGHT-'n fuh) *id.* went directly toward
"W'en 'e git tuh de big road, 'e straight'n fuh towng."
(When he reached the highway, he went directly toward town.)

strain
(STRAIN) *n.* train/-s
"De strain out 'e runnin'."
(The train is not on schedule.)

strance
(STRANCE) *n.* trance/-s
"'E stan' lukkuh 'e een uh strance."
(He looks like he is in a trance.)

strengk
(STRENGK) *n.* strength/-s
"Pa done lose 'e strengk; 'e dat ole."
(Father has lost his strength; he's that old.)

strick
(STRICK) *v.* stricken; affected
"Bill strick wid uh t'reat ub uh stroke."
(Bill was stricken with the

threat of a stroke.)

'stroy'd
(STROYD) *v.* destroy/-s/-ed/-ing
"De harricane 'stroy'd we house."
(The hurricane destroyed our house.)

struct'd
(STRUCTD) *v.* strike/-s, struck, striking
"Uh snake struct'd Pa ole houn' dog."
(A snake struck Father's old hound dog.)

stubbunt
(STUB-bunt) *adj.* stubborn
"Dat mule stubbunt 'tell 'e yent wu't'."
(That mule is so stubburn, he is worthless.)

study 'e head
(stud-y e HEAD) *id.* study his/her/its head; think, thought, thinking
"'E yent study 'e head 'bout wu'k."
(He is not thinking about work.)

suhstiffikut
(suh-STIFF-i-kut) *n.* certificate
"De doctuh g'em suhstiffikut suh 'e waccinate."
(The doctor gave him a certificate saying he had been vaccinated.)

'suade
(SUADE) *v.* persuade/-s/-ed/-ing
"'E ma try fuh 'suade de gal fuh gone."
(Her mother tried to persuade the girl to go.)

suck 'e teet'
(suck e TEET) *id.* suck his/her teeth; make a sucking sound by drawing breath between the teeth—implies disregard or impertinence
"De gal suck 'e 'teet' en' ent pay 'e ma no min'."
(The girl made a sucking sound with her teeth and completely disregarded her mother.)

suffuhrate
(suf-fuh-RATE) *v.* separate/-s/-ed/-ing
"Jake en' 'e lawfully lady done suffuhrate."
(Jake and his wife have already separated.)

suh
(SUH) *n.* sir/-s
"Yaas, suh, de strain done gone."
(Yes, sir, the train has already gone.)

suh
(SUH) *v.* say/-s, said, saying
"'E suh de strain done gone."
(He said the train had already gone.)

sukkle
SUK-kle) *v.* circle/-s/-ed/-ing
"T'ree bu'd duh sukkle een de element."
(Three birds are circling in the sky.)

sukkuh
(SUK-kuh) *id.* contraction of same lukkuh
"'E tas'e shaa'p, sukkuh aacit."
(It has a sharp taste, like acid.)

summuch
(SUM-much) *adv.* many
"Summuch dem gwine nawt'."
(Many of them are going north.)

sump'n'nurruh
(sump-'N-NUR-RUH) *n.* something or other
"Sump'n'nurruh bin hide een de bresh."
(Something or other was hiding in the bushes.)

sunhot
(sun-HOT) *n.* sunshine; heat from the sun
"De sunhot gwi' 'cawch 'e hide."
(The sunshine is going to scorch his skin.)

sun-lean
(sun-LEAN) *n.* sundown; dusk, twilight
"Us gwi' walk 'tell sun-lean."
(We are going to walk until the sun goes down.)
NOTE: SEE ALSO *DUS'*, *FUS' DAA'K*, AND *CANDL' LIGHT'N*.

sup'shun
(SUP-shun) *n.* substance (used primarily when referring to food value)
"Dat soup ent hab sup'shun."
(That soup does not have any substance.)

sutt'nly
(SUTT-n-ly) *adv.* certainly
"Dem han' sutt'nly lazy en' good fuh nutt'n."
(Those hands are certainly lazy and good for nothing.)

swaytuh Gawd
(SWAY-tuh GAWD) *interj.* swear to God
"Uh swaytuh Gawd 'e true."
(I swear to God it's true.)

sweetmout'um
(SWEET-mout-um) *id.* flatter/-s/-ed/-ing his/her/them
"'E sweetmout'-um and baig 'tel dey g'em de money."
(He flattered them and begged until they gave him the money.)

swell-up
(SWELL-up) *v.* grow larger; swell with anger
"'E jaw swell-up; 'e dat bex."
(Her jaw swelled up; she was that vexed.)

swif'
(SWIF) *adv.* swiftly
"'E run dat swif', 'e done git yuh."
(He ran so swiftly, he is here already.)

swimp
(SWIMP) *n.* shrimp/-s
"Dem cas' t'ree time en' git
'nuf swimp."
(They cast the net three times
and got enough shrimp.)

swinge
(SWINGE) *n.* singe/-s/-ed/-ing
"Attuh oonuh done pick de
chickin, mus' swinge 'um
good-fashi'n 'fo' 'e cook."
(After you have plucked the
chicken, you must singe it
well before it is cooked.)

swink
(SWINK) *v.* shrink/-s, shrunk,
shrinking
"De chile dress done swink."
(The child's dress has shrunk.)

swonguh
(SWONG-uh) *adj.* swanky;
boastful
"'E uh soon-man 'cep'm 'e too
swonguh."
(He is a stylish man but he is
too boastful.)

T

taar
(TAAR) n. tar
"Chink up de hole wid taar."
(Fill the hole with tar.)

taas'
(TAAS) *n.* task
"Uh done finish de taas'."
(I have already completed the
task.)

'tacktid
(TACK-tid) *v.* attack/-s/-ed/
-ing
"De rokkoon 'tacktid de houn'
dog."
(The raccoon attacked the
hound dog.)

'taguhnize
(TAG-o-nize) *v.* antagonize/-s/
-ed/-ing
"De chillun eenjy 'taguhnize 'e
ma."
(The children enjoy antagoniz-
ing their mother.)

talluh
(TAL-luh) *n.* tallow
"Mus' sabe de talluh fuh mek
candle."
(You must save the tallow to
make candles.)

tallygraf
(TAL-LY-graf) *n.* telegram/-s
"Pa sen' tallygraf, suh 'e git
tuh New Yawk."
(Father sent a telegram saying
that he had reached New
York.)

tallyfon
(TAL-LY-fon) *n.* telephone/-s
"Dat tallyfon too tangledy."
(That telephone is too confus-
ing.)

tangledy
(TAN-GLE-dy) *adj.* tangled;
confusing
"De jedge wu'd too tangledy."
(The judge's words are too
confusing.)

'tarrygate
(TAR-RY-gate) *v.* interrogate/-s/-ed/-ing
"'E done tarrygate'um 'tell 'e yent know wuh 'e duh talk 'bout."
(He has questioned him until he no longer knows what he is saying.)

tarrypin
(TAR-RY-pin) *n.* terrapin/-s
"Tarrypin good fuh mek soup."
(A terrapin makes good soup.)

tas'e
(TASE) *v.* taste/-s/-ed/-ing
"Tarrypin tas'e same lukkuh chickin."
(Terrapin tastes just like chicken.)

tas'e 'e mout
(TASE e mout) *id.* put/-s a good taste in the mouth
"Bakin tas'e 'e mout'."
(Bacon puts a good taste in the mouth.)

tayre
(TAY-re) *v.* tear/-s, tore, tearing
"De baby tayre 'e shu't."
(The baby tore his shirt.)

tayre
(TAY-re) *adv.* torn
"De baby shu't tayre."
(The baby's shirt is torn.)

teet'ache
(TEET-ache) *n.* toothache
"'E cyan' eat; 'e hab uh teet'ache."
(He can't eat; he has a toothache.)

tek
(TEK) *v.* take/-s, took, taking
"'E tek t'ree dose ub de med'sin."
(He took three doses of the medicine.)

tek 'e foot een 'e han'
(tek e FOOT een e han) *id.* take his foot in his hand; travel quickly; leave hurriedly
"De man tek 'e foot een 'e han' w'en de gal aa'gyfy wid'um."
(The man left hurriedly when the girl began to argue with him.)

tek 'e place
(tek e PLACE) *id.* take his/her place; sit in his/her usual place
"De gal tek 'e place wid de fam'bly een chu'ch."
(The girl sat with the family in church.)

tek 'e pledjuh
(tek e PLED-juh) *id.* take time for pleasure; enjoy
"Jake tek 'e pledjuh duh fish."
(Jake enjoyed fishing.)

tek'um fuh mek fun
(TEK-um fuh mek FUN) *id.* ridiculed or poked fun at someone or something
"'E do'um too bad, 'e tek'um

fuh mek fun."
(He treated them without respect; he made fun of them.)

tek 'way
(TEK-way) *id.* take/s away; when used with *head*, implies the brain is not functioning properly
"'E head tek'way."
(He is demented; he has lost his reasoning power.)

tek wid um
(tek WID um) *id.* taken with him/her/it/them
"'E so tek wid um 'e cyan' res'."
(He is so taken with her, he can't sleep.)

'tel
(TEL) *adv.* until
"Set yuh 'tell uh git't'ru."
(Sit here until I get through.)

'ten'
(TEN) *v.* attend/s/ed/ing
"'Ten' tuh de baby!"
(Attend to the baby!)

'ten'
(TEN) *v.* intend/-s/-ed/-ing
"Uh yent 'ten' fuh do'um."
(I didn't intend to do it.)

t'engk
(TENGK) *v.* thank/-s/-ed/-ing
"'E t'engk'um fuh de gif'."
(She thanked them for the gift.)

tenight
(te-NIGHT) *adv.* tonight
"Dem gwine tenight."
(They are going tonight.)

'tenshun
(TEN-shun) *v.* attention
"'E yent pay um no 'tenshun."
(He did not pay them any attention.)

tetch
(TETCH) *n.* touch; a small amount
"T'row uh tetch ob salt cross'um."
(Put a little salt on it.)

'tettuh
(TET-tuh) *n.* potato/-es
(Bile de 'tettuh 'tell 'e done."
(Boil the potato until it is done.)

t'ick
(TICK) *adj.* thick
"De bresh bin berry t'ick."
(The bushes were very thick.)

t'icket
(TICK-it) *n.* thicket/-s
"Dey gone blackberry t'icket."
(They went to the blackberry thicket.)

tie 'e mout'
(tie e MOUT) *id.* shut his/her mouth
"Mek dat gal ent tie 'e mout'?"
(Why doesn't that girl shut her mouth?)

t'ief
(TIEF) *v.* [thief]; steal/-s, stole, stealing
"Bubbuh t'ief de hog."
(Brother stole the hog.)

t'ing
(TING) *n.* thing
"Dat t'ing do'um bad.
(That thing had a bad effect on him.)

'ting
(TING) *v.* sting/-s, stung, stinging
"Anch 'ting de baby bumbo."
(Ants stung the baby on his rump.)

t'ink
(TINK) *v.* think/-s, thought, thinking
"Uh t'ink uh shum."
(I think I saw them.)

t'irteen
(TIR-teen) *adj.* thirteen
"De sow hab t'irteen pig."
(The sow had thirteen pigs.)

t'irty
(TIRT-y) *adj.* thirty
"'E done lib yuh dese t'irty yeah."
(He has lived here thirty years.)

todduh
(TOD-DUH) *adj.* the other
"'E dance mo' bettuh dan todduh man."
(He dances better than the other man.)

NOTE: *TODDUH* AND *TUDDUH* ARE USED INTERCHANGEABLY.

too
(TOO) *adv.* very
"Uh too glad fuh shum."
(I'm very glad to see them.)

tossle
(TOSS-le) *n.* tassle/-s
"Sandy hat hab tossle 'pun'top'um."
(Sanda's hat has a tassle on top of it.)

tote
(TOTE) *v.* carry/-ies/-ed/-ing
"De gal tote watuh 'pun'top 'e haid."
(The girl carries water on her head.)

t'ous'n'
(TOUS-'n) *n.* thousand
"De teachuh laa'n'um fuh count tuh t'ous'n'."
(The teacher taught them to count to a thousand.)

towng
(TOWNG) *n.* town/-s
"Uh buy um tuh towng."
(I bought it in town.)

trabble
(TRAB-ble) *v.* travel/-s/-ed/-ing
"Dem trabble duh big road."
(They traveled the highway.)

'traight
(TRAIGHT) *adv.* straight
"Dem gone 'traight to towng."

(They went straight to town.)

t'rash
(TRASH) *v.* thrash
"'E busy duh t'rash w'eat."
(He is busy thrashing wheat.)

t'rashuh-bu'd
(TRASH-uh-bud) *n.* thrush or thrasher [bird]
"De t'rashuh-bu'd sing in de mawnin'."
(The thrush sang in the morning.)

t'read
(TREAD) *n.* thread/-s
"Ma gone sto' fuh git han' t'read."
(Mother has gone to the store to get sewing thread.)

tredjuh
(TRED-juh) *v.* treasure/-s/-ed/-ing
"Ma tredjuh de ole chany."
(Mother treasured the old china.)

t'ree
(TREE) *adj.* three
"De chile een 'e t'ree yeah."
(The child is three years old.)

t'ree-time
(TREE-time) *adv.* third time
"Ma done call'um fuh de t'ree-time."
(Mother called them for the third time.)

'tretch
(TRETCH) *v.* stretch/-es/-ed/-ing
"De ole dog 'tretch en' 'cratch 'ese'f."
(The old dog stretched and scratched himself.)

'tring
(TRING) *n.* string/-s
"De crab net mek ub 'tring."
(The crab net is made of string.)

t'roat
(TROAT) *n.* throat/-s
"Me t'roat so'."
(My throat is sore.)

t'row
(ROW) *v.* throw/-s, threw, throwing
"T'row de ball yuh!"
(Throw the ball here!)

t'rowbone
(TRO-bone) *id.* play dice; shoot craps
"'Lijah berry lub fuh t'rowbone."
(Elijah very much loves to play dice.)

t'row 'e yeye
(TRO e eye) *id.* throw his/her eye; look at carefully; search
"De gal t'row 'e yeye 'pun 'top de mens."
(The girl looked closely at the men.)

t'row'um 'way
TROW um way) *id.* throw him/her/them away; divorced him/her

"'E wife t'row'um 'way."
(His wife divorced him.)

t'ru
(TRU) *adj.* through
"'E gone t'ru' de gyap."
(She went through the opening in the fence.)

t'row 'e woice
(throw e WOICE) *id.* [throw his/her voice]; sing, sang, sung
"De bu'd t'row 'e woice all t'ru de night."
(The bird sang all through the night.)

trus'
(TRUS) *v.* trust/-s/-ed/-ing
"Pa yent trus' de boat fuh gone een um. De boat ent specify."
(Father doesn't trust the boat for use. It isn't seaworthy.

trus'-me-Gawd
(TRUS-me-GAWD) *n.* an undependabe homemade boat
"'E yent gwine 'long de trus'-me-Gawd; de ole canoe mo' safe."
(He isn't going in the homemade boat; the old canoe is safer.)

trute
(TRUTE) *n.* truth/-s
"Tell you de trute, you cyan' git dey f'um yuh!"
(To tell you the truth, you can't get there from here.

trute-mout'
(TRUTE-mout) *n.* a dependable person; one who tells the truth
"Mistuh Noruh bin de onlies trute-mout' een de w'ull."
Mister Noah was the only dependable person in the world.)

tuckrey
(TUCK-rey *n.* turkey/-s
"De tuckrey ju'k out 'e fedduh; 'e dat bex!"
(The turkey jerked out his feathers; he was that vexed.)

tuh
(TUH) *prep.* to; at; in; on
"Uh gwine tuh chu'ch."
(I am going to church.)

tuh dat
(TUH dat) *adv.* to that [degree]
"'E duh nyam dry cawn hom'ny; 'e hongry tuh dat!"
(He is eating plain hominy, with no butter or gravy; he is that hungry!)

tuhgedduh
(TUH-ged-duh) *adv.* together
"Alltwo dem wu'k tuhgedduh."
(They both worked together.)

tuhreckly
(TUH-reck-ly) *adv.* directly; soon
"Uh gwine home tuhreckly."
(I'm going home soon.)

tummuch
(TUM-much) *adv.* too much; very much
"'E tummuch wu'k fuh cook!"
(It is too much work to cook.)

tu'n
(TUN) *v.* turn/-s/-ed/-ing
"Dem tu'n 'roun' en' gone."
(They turned around and left.)

t'unduh
(TUN-duh) *n.* thunder
"De light'nin' flesh en' de t'unduh roll."
(The lightning flashed and the thunder rolled.)

tu'nup
(TUN-up) *n.* turnip/-s
"Ma plant two row ub tu'nip."
(Mother planted two rows of turnips.)

tup'mtime
(TUP-m-time) *n.* turpentine
"Tup'mtine en' suguh cyo' uh col'."
(Turpentine mixed with sugar will cure a cold.)

T'ursd'y
(TURS-dy) *PN.* Thursday
"'E bin sick sence T'ursd'y."
(He has been sick since Thursday.)

tush
(TUSH) *n.* tusk
"De wil' hog bruk one 'e tush."
(The wild hog broke one of his tusks.)

t'u'sty
(TUS-ty) *adj.* thirsty
"'E bin sick sence T'ursd'y."
(He has been sick since Thursday.)

twelb
(TWELB) *adj.* twelve
"Twelb boy duh race."
(Twelve boys are racing.)

twis'-mout'
(TWIS-mout) *adj.* twisted mouth; deformed mouth
"De baby twis-mout'."
(The baby has a deformed mouth.)

twis'up
(twiss-up) *v.* twisted up; deformed
"Pa twis'up wid de mi'sry een 'e j'int.
(Father has arthritis.)

two place
(TWO place) *id.* second place
"Een de two place, time fuh gone!"
(In the second place, it's time for me to go.)

two-time-one-gun
(TWO-time-one-gun) *n.* a double barrelled shotgun

two-t'ree
(TWO-tree) *adj.* several; two or three
"Two-t'ree gal bin dey dey."
(Two or three girls were there.)

U

ub
(UB) *prep.* of
"'E one ub we people."
(He is one of us.)

uh
(UH) *pron.* I
"Uh yeddy um."
(I hear them.)

uh
(UH) *adj.* a; an
"Uh dog bin dey dey."
(A dog was right there.)

uhlly
(UHL-LY) *adj.* early
"'E git yuh uhlly dis mawnin'."
(He got here early this morning.)

um
(UM) *pron.* him/her/it/them
"Uh yeddy um!"
(I heard them.)

us
(US) *pron.* we; our
"Dem nyam us meat."
(They ate our meat.)

W

wabe
(WABE) *n.* wave/-s
"De wabe gone 'cross de boat."
(The waves went over the boat.)

wabe
(WABE) *v.* wave/-s/-ed/-ing
"'E wabe tuh 'e ma."
(He waved to his mother.)

waccinate
(WAC-cin-ate) *v.* vaccinate/-s/-ed/-ing
"De doctuh done waccinate de chillun."
(The doctor has vaccinated the children.)

waggybone
(WAG-GY-bone) *n.* vagabond/-s
"Ma suh mus' don' trus' dem waggybone."
(Mother said you must not trust those vagabonds.)

wah
(WA) *n.* war/-s
"Slab'ry gone out attuh de wah."
(There was no more slavery after the war.)

wais'
(WAIS) *n.* waist
"De dress gedduh tuh wais'."
(The dress is gathered at the waist.)

wallyubble
(wal-ly-UB-BLE) *adj.* valuable
"De man los' 'e wallyable mule."
(The man lost his valuable mule.)

wan'
(WAN) v. want/-s/-ed/-ing
"Uh wan' gone home!"
(I want to go home!)

w'ary
(WA-RY) adj. weary
"Uh too w'ary fuh gone."
(I'm too weary to go.)

wase
(WASE) n. vase/-s
"Pit de rose een de wase and set um 'pun'top de table."
(Put the rose in a vase and set it on the table.)

was'e
(WASE) v. waste/-s/-ed/-ing
"Bile de crab so dey yent was'e."
(Boil the crabs so they are not wasted.)

watuh
(WA-tuh) n. water
"Tote de watuh tuh de han'."
(Carry the water to the workers.)

watuhmilyun
(wa-tuh-MIL-YUN) n. watermelon
"Oonuh t'ief dat watuhmilyun, enty?"
(You stole that watermelon, didn't you?)

wawm
(WAWM) adj. warm
"Light de fiah fuh we wawm."
(Make a fire so that we can be warm.)

wawn
(WAWN) v. warn/-s/-ed/-ing
"Uh wawn'um mus' don' nyam de pie."
(I warned them not to eat the pie.)

wawss'
(WAWSS) n. wasp/-s
"Ma suh mus' lef' de wawss' nes' 'lone."
(Mother said to leave the wasp's nest alone.)

we
(WE) pron. our, us
"Dat one fuh we, enty?"
(That one's for us, isn't it?)

w'eat
(WEAT) n. wheat
"De w'eat sell fuh 'nuf money."
(The wheat sold for plenty of money.)

wedd'n'
(WEDD-'n) n. wedding/-s
"All ub we gwine tuh de wedd'n'."
(All of us are going to the wedding.)

wedduh
(WED-duh) v. [weather]; indicates inclimate weather conditions: storming, raining, snowing, etc.
"'E duh wedduh!"
(It is storming.)

w'edduh
(WED-duh) conj. whether

"Uh yent know w'edduh dem gwine."
(I don't know whether they are going.)

w'eel
(WEEL) *n.* wheel/-s
"De cyaa't w'eel bruk."
(The cart wheel is broken.)

w'eelego gal
(WEEL-e-go-gal) *id.* an obese girl; a big girl
"Dat uh w'eelego gal!"
("That is a big girl!)

wegitubble
WEG-it-UB-BLE) *n.* vegetable/-s
"Ma sell 'e wegitubble tuh towng."
(Mother sold her vegetables in town.)

weh
(WEH) *adv.* where
"Weh 'e is?"
(Where is he?)

wehebbuh
(WEH-eb-buh) *adv.* wherever
"Wehebbuh 'e lib, us gwine dey dey."
(Wherever he lives, we are going there.)

weh 'e lib
(weh e LIB) *id.* obsessed by an idea or thought
"Bittle weh 'e lib."
(Food is all she thinks about.)

w'en
(WEN) *adv.* when
"W'en 'e gwine?"
(When is she going?)

w'enebbuh
(WEN-eb-buh) *adv.* whenever
"W'enebbuh 'e git't'ru wid 'e wu'k, 'e lef'."
(Whenever she gets through with her work, she leaves.)

We'n'sd'y
(WENS-dy) *n.* Wednesday
"De fambly lef' home We'n'sd'y."
The family left home Wednesday.)

we'own
(WE-own) *pron.* our own; ours
"De cat we'own."
(The cat is ours.)

werry
(WER-ry) *adv.* very
"Uh werry glad fuh shum!"
(I'm very glad to see them.)

we'se'f
(WE-sef) *pron.* ourselves
"We'se'f gone."
(We went ourselves.)

wet-drought
(WET-drought) *n.* excessively wet weather
"De wet-drought spile de wegitubble."
(The extremely wet weather spoiled the vegetables.)

w'ich
(WICH) *pron.* which
"W'ich one dem ent git yuh?"
(Which one of them did not get here?)

wickitty
(WICK-it-ty) *n.* wickedness
"Dem gwi' punish fuh dem wickitty."
(They are going to be punished for their wickedness.)

wid
(WID) *prep.* with
"De baby come 'long wid um."
(The baby came with them.)

'w'ile
(WILE) *adv.* awhile
"Attuh 'w'ile dem gone home."
(After awhile they went home.)

win'
(WIN) *n.* wind
"De win' fetch de smell ub de maa'sh."
(The wind brings the smell of the marsh.)

wine
(WINE) *n.* vine/-s
"De cow tangledy up een de wine."
(The cow is completely tangled in the vines.)

winiguh
(WIN-e-guh) *n.* vinegar
"Apple good fuh mek winiguh."
(Apples are good for making vinegar.)

wissit
(WISS-it) *n.* visit/-s
"We frien' come fuh wissit."
(Our friend came for a visit.)

w'ite
(WITE) *adj.* white
"Bile de clothes 'tel dem w'ite."
(Boil the clothes until they are white.)

wranch
(WRANCH) *n.* wrench/-es
"Pa fix de plow wid de wranch."
(Father fixed the plow with the wrench.)

wrop
(WROP) *v.* wrap/-s/-ed/-ing
"Wrop up de baby good-fashi'n."
(Wrap the baby well.)

wu'd
(WUD) *n.* word/-s
"Wu'd git 'roun' 'bout de paa'ty."
(Word got around about the party.)

wuffuh
(WUFF-uh) *adv.* [what for]; why; for what purpose
"Wuffuh dem duh talk 'bout um?"
(Why did they talk about it?)

wuh
(WUH) *adv.* what; that; who
"Wuh dat is?"
(What is that?)

wu'k
(WUK) *v.* work/s/ed/ing
"'E duh wu'k."
(He is working.)

wu'll
(wul) *n.* world/s
"Gawd mek de wu'll."
(God made the world.)

wurrum
(WUR-rum) *n.* worm/s
"Wurrum dey een de cawn yeah."
(Worms are in the corn ears.)

wusshup
(WUS-shup) *v.* worship/-s/-ed/-ing
"Dem duh wusshup, duh clap, en' shout tuh de meet'n'."
(They are worshipping, clapping, and shouting at the meeting.)

wussuh
(WUSS-uh) *adv.* worse
"Dat gal sing wussuh dan de nex' gal."
(That girl doesn't sing as well as the other girl.)

wu't'
(WUT) *n.* worth; value
"Dat lan' ent wu't'."
(That land has no value.)

w'y'mek'so
(wy-MEK-so) *id.* Why? What makes it so?
"Dat lan' ent wu't'. W'y'mek'so?"
(That land has no value. Why?)

Y

yaa'd
(YAAD) *n.* yard/-s
"Ma suh mus' clean de yaa'd.
(Mother said to clean the yard.)

yaa'd-aig
(YAAD-aig) *n.* yard egg; egg/-s laid by a hen in the yard
"Gedduh de yaa'd-aig."
(Gather the eggs from the yard.)

yaa'd-chile
(YAAD-chile) *n.* a child old enough to play in the yard
"Gib de yaa'd-chile 'e bittle."
(Give the child in the yard his food.)

yaa'n
(YAAN) *n.* yarn/-s
"De scaa'f mek ub yaa'n."
(The scarf is made of yarn.)

yeah
(YE-AH) *n.* ear/-s, as of corn; year/-s
"'E bile ten yeah ub cawn."
(She boiled ten ears of corn.)

yeddy
(YED-DY) *v.* hear/-s, heard, hearing
"Uh yeddy um, but Uh yent shum."
(I heard them, but I did not see them.)

Uh yeddy ax duh talk.
id. I hear an ax talking.
(Someone is chopping wood.)

yent
(YENT) *v.* is/are, do/did, was/were, am not
"'E yent gwine."
(He is not going.)
NOTE: ENT BECOMES YENT WHEN PRECEDED BY A VOWEL.

yez
(YEZ) *n.* ear/-s
"Uh yent b'leebe me yez."
(I don't believe my ears.)

yistiddy
(YIS-tid-dy) *n.* yesterday
"'E come home yistiddy."
(She came home yesterday.)

you'own
(YOU-own) *pron.* your own; yours
"Dem shoesh you'own, enty?"
(Those shoes are yours, are they not?)

yuh
(YUH) *adv.* here
"Yuh uh is."
(Here I am.)

Z

'zackly
(ZACK-ly) *adv.* exactly
"'E tell'um 'zackly huffuh do um."
(He told them exactly how to do it.)

'zammin
(ZAM-MIN) *v.* examine/-s/-ed/-ing
(De doctuh 'zammin de baby."
(The doctor examined the baby.)

zoon'n
(ZOON-'n) *v.* move directly
"Ben zoon'n fuh 'e pay."
(Ben came in directly for his pay.)
NOTE: THIS IS AN ONOMATOPOEIC EXPRESSION, THE SOUND IMITATING THAT MADE BY A BEE.

ABOUT THE AUTHOR

VIRGINIA MIXSON GERATY lived for more than fifty years in the Yonges Island area of the South Carolina lowcountry where she learned to speak and write the Gullah language. Because of her continuing work in preserving the language, Ms. Geraty was awarded in 1995 the honorary degree of Doctor of Humane Letters by the College of Charleston.

Ms. Geraty's previous publications include

- **PORGY: A GULLAH VERSION**
  adapted from the original play *Porgy* by Dorothy and DuBose Heyward

- **PORGY: A GULLAH VERSION**
  videotape based on the book

- **BITTLE EN' T'ING': GULLAH COOKING WITH MAUM CHRISH'**
  recipes with English translations

- **CHARLESTON'S HIGHLIGHTS, SIDELIGHTS & SHADOWS**
  a history of Charleston, South Carolina, on audio cassette tape

- **MAUM CHRISH' CHAA'STUN: A GULLAH STORY**
  an audio cassette tape featuring stories of Charleston told in Gullah

- **GULLAH NIGHT BEFORE CHRISTMAS**
  a Gullah version of the famous poem

To order books and videotapes by Virginia Geraty, call

Sandlapper Publishing Co., Inc.
1–800–849–7263